D0065899

FIVE FROGS
ON A LOG

FIVE FROGS ON A LOG

A CEO's Field Guide to Accelerating
the Transition in Mergers, Acquisitions,
and Gut Wrenching Change

Mark L. Feldman and
Michael F. Spratt

PRICEWATERHOUSECOOPERS

HarperBusiness
A Division of HarperCollins*Publishers*

HarperCollins books may be purchased for educational, business, or sales promotional use. For information please write: Special Markets Department, Harper-Collins Publishers, Inc., 10 East 53rd Street, New York, NY 10022.

FIRST EDITION

Designed by Deirdre Amthor

Library of Congress Cataloging-in-Publication Data

Feldman, Mark L., 1947–
    Five frogs on a log: a CEO's field guide to accelerating the transition in
mergers, acquisitions, and gut wrenching change/Mark L. Feldman, Michael F.
Spratt.—1st ed.
       p. cm.
    ISBN 0-88730-981-X
    1. Consolidation and merger of corporations—Management. 2. Corporate
reorganizations—Management. I. Spratt Michael Frederick. II. Title
HD2746.5.F448 1999
658.1'—dc21   98-29088

99 00 01 02 03 ❖/RRD 10 9 8 7 6 5 4 3 2 1

A child's riddle:

Five frogs are sitting on a log.
Four decide to jump off. How many are left?
Answer: five.
Why?
Because deciding and doing are not the same thing.

"The race is not always to the swift, nor the battle to the strong—but that's the way to bet."

—*Damon Runyon*

Contents

Acknowledgments

One of the most difficult decisions we faced in writing this book was choosing to leave behind some of our favorite stories and characters. Inspired by our clients, drawn from our own fevered fantasies and snatched from the fertile minds of our family, friends, and colleagues, many of the favorite apocryphal tales we tell to audiences—of raccoons with sugar cubes, big elephants and short spears, abominable snowmen, leaky boats, boa constrictors, and the Daffy Duck syndrome—became sad casualties of editorial privilege. To their fans, we offer our gratitude and our condolences. They forfeited precious space so that the stories of bullfrogs, boobies, mole hill men, camels, dogs, cats, paperboys, tow trucks, and turtles might survive.

Such is the cruelty of the literary arts.

No less frustrating was our inability to cram between the covers of this book, the names of all the people who stimulated our thinking, offered much needed criticism, contributed time, and toiled selflessly to help create what you hold in your hands.

We owe our sincerest thanks to many people.

To our partners and colleagues at PricewaterhouseCoopers who have enthusiastically embraced the value proposition described in this book.

To Reed Keller and Ray Ranelli who shared our vision and provided crucial early support.

To Don Shay, Greg Peterson, Keith Humphries, Bob Filek, Ruth Hunt, Rich Carson, Mark Moscarello, Rita Gail Johnson, Drew Koecher, Kevin Scott, Mark Dufilho, Barbara Kraft, Terry Sherwood, Kathleen Collins, Kathy Walgamuth, Joe Mallahan, Maureen Tickner, Chuck Butler, Frank Brown, John Liu, Dwayne Watts, Melea Lusk, and the other PricewaterhouseCoopers partners and consultants who have committed themselves to The Accelerated Transition® business team.

To Valerie Van Sickle, Doug Murata, Bob Patrick and Walt Jacobs of The Rubicon Group, who invested in the concept when it was an emerging proposition.

To Al Riordan, our mentor and longtime friend, who taught us to stretch ourselves and our ideas.

To Jan Emanuel, our dedicated assistant, who continues to steer us through the administrative minefields.

To Jean Lin, our intrepid researcher and closet critic, who stalked data and offered praise when we needed it and blunt honesty whether we wanted it or not.

And to our collective family, Adele, Ann, Sean, Pat, John, Keiko, Fred, Ada, Sandra, Shahn, and Kris, who have given us strength, joy, and reason to try.

For over fifteen years, the two of us have worked together to form and hone the value proposition presented in this book. We feel fortunate to have experienced both the power and the pleasure of true creative collaboration. We no longer can trace our ideas, concepts, or words to one or the other of us.

So, in the future, if by some chance you bump into either one of us at a conference, or at the airport, or on the street, and you choose to challenge a point we have made in this book . . . remember the other guy wrote that part.

Foreword

Mergers, Acquisitions, and Large-Scale Change

Who's kidding whom? The history of corporate change is replete with false starts, missed targets, and dramatic disappointments. And as more and more business leaders find themselves managing a merger, acquisition, or other large-scale restructuring, the threats to personal and reputational capital loom large.

Nowhere is this more apparent than in mergers and acquisitions. We recall the client who referred to his investment bankers as 2 percent country gentlemen and 98 percent rogue used-car salesmen. The experience started out easy and ego-pleasing, with its aura of big money, immediate growth, and instant competitive advantage seasoned with a touch of colonialism; cheering from the sidelines, the investment bankers promised much and pocketed more. What the bankers didn't—and rarely ever—discuss were the jolts, curves, and emotional potholes on the rough road ahead.

"If only I knew then what I know now, I never would have done the deal," he moaned. "When I add the cost of the deal to the post-deal downturn and the opportunities we lost because we were distracted and loaded down with debt, it's clear that U.S. Treasuries would have been a better investment. But acquiring seemed so easy. You buy it one day, and it's yours the next."

He was right. Acquiring is easy. Owning is hard. Big organizational changes offer the opportunity to reap big losses. Acquisitions are never risk-free. Integration is never seamless. Expectations always exceed actual gains.

Whether you're buying another company or acquiring a new vision of the future, this is a time of relentless change. Increasingly, the companies that win are those that learn faster, act quicker, and adapt sooner. They compress time by making and executing early, informed decisions about economic value creation, ruthless prioritization, and focused resource allocation. They use these decisions to take early, firm stands on management deployment, organization structure, and culture. Their actions are increasingly linked to long-term, sustained economic value creation.

The principles and practices described in this book chart the path. They apply to a wide range of business and operational problems: from accelerating the development of a new product to merging two companies; from creating a service-driven culture to repositioning a business in a whole new marketplace. However, the most rigorous test of these principles is how they handle the turbulence surrounding mergers, acquisitions, and gut-wrenching changes.

Navigating a major transition is a race against time. Executives quickly discover that they are late even before they get started. Everything becomes a priority. Years of deployment decisions must be made in days. There are hundreds of questions and only a handful of vague answers. Nobody is doing his or her job effectively. Customers are being neglected. Productivity is plummeting. Chaos is spreading like wildfire.

These special situations magnify the operational, organizational, and human resource problems facing executives who are expected to work miracles. Navigating a major transition is a race against time. Executives quickly discover that they are late even before they get started. Everything becomes a priority. Years of deployment decisions must be made in days. There are hundreds of questions and only a handful of vague answers. Nobody is doing his or her job effec-

tively. Customers are being neglected. Productivity is plummeting. Chaos is spreading like
wildfire.

This is the environment into
which the executive team is
thrust. A beleaguered group who
set aside other business concerns
to do the deal, they are now faced
with a backlog of decisions to

> **This is not the time to call up the latest management fad. It's the time for a financially driven, solidly pragmatic, results-oriented approach to accelerating change—an approach that is focused on creating economic value and stakeholder opportunity.**

make and a surplus of new challenges to tackle. They struggle for control
and search for direction. They have little patience for process, no tolerance for wasting time, and a single-minded focus on eliminating the stag-
gering costs associated with every day of delay. This is not the time to call
up the latest management fad. It's the time for a financially driven, solidly
pragmatic, results-oriented approach to *accelerating* change—an approach that is focused on creating economic value and stakeholder op-
portunity.The accelerated transition approach described in this book is a
distinctive proposition for generating momentum, capturing early wins,
and creating shareholder value. While the approach has been successful
in a wide range of environments, it has proved to be most valuable in the
hostile and unforgiving world of mergers, acquisitions, and large-scale
change. It is for this reason that most of the stories and examples are
drawn from this environment.

The Salado River

*The Seven Deadly Sins
of Transitions*

Sabinas, Mexico, September 6, 1960. An unusually heavy thunderstorm drenches the fertile farmland on the eastern slopes of the Sierra Madres. The sheer volume of water filling hundreds of small creeks and tributaries causes the Salado River to swell. A few small concrete dams built across the river as part of a long-term plan to provide water for irrigation and livestock quickly fill up and begin to overflow. Even though there is little threat of serious flooding, the citizens of Sabinas face another challenge. You see, in Sabinas the top of the dam also serves as the bridge connecting the small rural community to the more populated cities of Monclova, Saltillo, and Monterrey. Today, however, few people are crossing the hundred-yard stretch of concrete now submerged under two feet of the Salado River.

The overflow presents a minor inconvenience to the local residents and a major problem to any traveler passing through Sabinas. By the next day the water level should drop, allowing safe passage to all who wish to cross the Salado River. But today only large trucks and buses are successfully fording the river.

Two enterprising local residents with tow trucks have set up camp on the southern riverbank, hoping to sell their towing services to a few stranded gringos attempting to return to the United States by way of

Piedras Negras. The southern side of the river is an ideal location for these entrepreneurs, who hope to make a month's wages for a few hours of easy work. The town, including one small hotel and two restaurants, sits on the northern side of the river. Those stranded on the southern side can return to the United States either by fording the river or by retracing their route to Saltillo or Monterrey and returning by way of Reynosa. All considered, the latter choice would take a whole extra day of travel.

Throughout the day, most travelers who approach from the south turn back and begin the long trek to Monterrey. However, a few stubborn drivers attempt a crossing without the aid of a tow truck. (The tow truck drivers, by the way, find this immensely entertaining; they're making side bets on how far each car will go before it stalls. Carlos is the big winner so far.)

Each of these independently minded drivers, determined to cross on his own, takes the same approach. He slowly eases the car into the current and then attempts to motor across as though the car were a small powerboat. After traveling twenty to thirty yards, the engine begins to sputter and then stalls. Waterlogged, stranded, and desperate, the driver then tries to negotiate a rescue fee with Carlos and his friend, while standing on the car roof, waving dollars and pesos, and screaming offers in a mixture of Spanish and English. All too willing to be of service, the tow truck drivers agree to assist for a small additional premium. After all, it is only fair that they be properly compensated for the added inconvenience of hitching a car while standing hip-deep in the Salado River.

By five in the afternoon, Carlos and his buddy have made a killing!

At about a quarter past five, a 1955 Chevrolet station wagon pulls up and stops next to Carlos's truck. The driver steps out and surveys the situation. Three small children and a wife sit in the car. The back is filled with luggage. This is the end of an economy vacation in Mexico, and the sun is beginning to set behind the Sierra Madres. Anxious to return home and low on cash and patience, the driver walks up to Carlos and asks what has happened to the road. In broken English, Carlos explains that the river has flooded and that it will be days before the water level drops. As a public service, he and his friend are assisting stranded travelers across the dangerous river for a small fee of twelve hundred pesos.

Just as Carlos begins to explain the terms of payment, another future customer edges up to the river. Carlos and the driver watch intently. This guy is taking a slightly different approach. Unlike the others, he enters the river with a little more speed and begins moving across, swerving around the stalled cars, and throwing off a small wake. It looks like he is going to make it across. Carlos frowns. The driver smiles. People watching on the north bank begin clapping and cheering in appreciation of this driver's cleverness and courage. Then, fewer than twenty yards from the northern edge of the river, the car hesitates, lurches forward, and then stops. The crowd sighs. The driver frowns. Carlos smiles.

"Twelve hundred pesos!" the waiting driver thinks to himself. "That's almost half our remaining cash." He walks back to the car and talks to his wife. For the next twenty minutes they talk and watch three more cars founder as they attempt to cross. The driver walks down to the river edge and watches Carlos rescue one car. A Greyhound bus pulls up, stops for a few seconds, and then charges across the river, nearly swamping Carlos and his new customer with its wake.

The driver looks back at his car. The kids are tired, and they want American hamburgers and milk that doesn't taste like a cow. His wife is fretting over being stranded in the middle of the river with three small children. They don't have money enough or time to take a daylong detour. This was not how he had planned to end their Mexican vacation.

Suddenly, without warning, he races back to the station wagon, jumps in, starts the engine, and looks in the rearview mirror. A large Greyhound bus rushes past. He guns the Chevy's engine and slips the clutch, throwing mud and gravel into the air. Carlos's friend covers his eyes and mouth.

The bus charges into the river with the Chevy wagon in hot pursuit. Carlos frowns as the bus and the Chevy pass him, nearly knocking him over with a three-foot wave. No more than six feet from the rear bumper of the bus, the Chevy is crossing in a wake of about eight inches of water. Looking out of the car are three wide-eyed, slack-jawed kids, one white-knuckled

mother, and one determined gringo who winks at Carlos as he passes.
Carlos's winning streak just came to an abrupt end.

Many companies approach major events like mergers or acquisitions
in the same way Carlos's customers entered the Salado River—slowly,
carefully, and, often, methodically determined to make it on their own.
Inevitably, these executives are unprepared for the chaos that follows.
Their best efforts to capture the new opportunities drive down performance and swamp the company.

Often they lose their composure and begin to thrash around for answers, frantically pursuing multiple paths in the hope that one will lead
to a face-saving solution. Many executives and boards try to scramble to
safety by concocting early exit strategies or recruiting celebrity executives, who with impunity can shift course and blame past executives for
the fallout. Unfortunately for most companies, Carlos and his tow truck
aren't around to haul them to safety. The towing service for companies
stranded in the middle of a merger or large-scale change extracts a much
higher fee. Smart boards and savvy institutional investors repossess your
car, lay off your family, and revoke your license to drive.

The Seven Deadly Sins in Implementing Transitions in Mergers, Acquisitions, and Gut Wrenching Change

As we learned on the Salado River, the formula for navigating the
torrent of change is deceptively simple: speed, focus, and momentum.
Chapters 1 through 3 detail the breadth of the problem. Chapters 4
through 12 offer solutions to avoiding the Seven Deadly Sins in implementing transitions.

Sin 1: Obsessive List Making

Within days of announcing a deal, the lords of infrastructure begin
compiling encyclopedic lists of things to do. As each day passes, new
transition teams are formed and more detail is added, until the master

list becomes a mind-numbing, morale-destroying, ego-deflating, knee-buckling litany of tasks. It consumes fifty typed pages backed by ten linear feet of Gantt charts—and seldom includes a revenue driver.

List-driven transitions are prolonged transitions. They dilute resources, undercapitalize efforts, and suboptimize results. By giving administrative detail and marginal cost-cutting the same priority as other value-creating actions, they retard progress, frustrate the workforce, and misallocate resources. Chapter 5 describes the value of focusing on the 20 percent of actions that are likely to drive 80 percent of the economic value with the highest probability of success, in the shortest possible timeframe.

Sin 2: Content-Free Communications

After announcing a deal or dramatic change, most communications tend to be 99 percent content-free. They consist primarily of hype and promotion and always produce more questions than answers.

Imagine you have acquired a company with ten thousand employees. Assume they feel relatively secure and spend only thirty minutes a day wondering, speculating, and trading gossip with others about their future. That comes to five thousand hours of lost productivity per day, twenty-five thousand hours a week and one hundred thousand hours a month for every month you leave them wondering and worrying.

Communication is a stabilizer. It keeps people focused and energized rather than confused and perplexed. When your stakeholders—employees, customers, suppliers, and investors—spend time worrying and wondering, they are not producing, buying, supplying, or investing. Chapter 6, "Windshield Watching in Seattle," and chapter 7, "No Secrets, No Surprises, No Hype, No Empty Promises," detail the process for securing the understanding and acceptance of the stakeholders, while mobilizing support.

Sin 3: Creating a Planning Circus

There is an old yachtsman's creed: "If you can't tie good knots, tie a lot of them." Many acquirers seem to apply this creed to transition teams. Out of some misguided sense of representational democracy, they form dozens of teams from both organizations to coordinate post-deal decisions and activities. The teams are organized into a byzantine structure that superimposes its own mass, complexity, and inertia on the transition. It slows progress and dilutes accountability. Chapter 8, "Five Frogs on a Log," covers the mechanics of launching small, fast-paced transition teams to expedite planning and execution.

Sin 4: Barnyard Behavior

Barnyard chickens have a well-defined pecking order. Mix in another flock and you disrupt the pecking order. The rules governing which bird can peck another become uncertain. Feathers fly. In the chaos, some are wounded. Some die.

CEOs seldom experience more pressure to clarify authority, control, and reporting relationships than after the announcement of a merger. Succumbing to pressure, their decisions favor form over function, titles over accountability, and hierarchy over role clarity. The result often leads to barnyard behavior and an early preoccupation with organization charts.

Complex roles and interrelationships are not clarified by publishing an organization chart. Organization charts say more about authority, status, power, and turf than about the flow of information and the way decisions are made. The barnyard behavior will continue, perhaps subtly, until roles and interrelationships are clarified. Chapter 9, "Acute Structural Anxiety," describes how to avoid stepping in barnyard residue.

Barnyard battles, though, are not limited to violations of the pecking order. Few things can make feathers fly faster than an empty promise to select the best practices from each party to a merger. Few things can produce a louder squawk than a clumsy attempt to ram together two sets of policies. Few things can raise hackles higher than a brutish downsizing or a flawed cost-reduction strategy that sacrifices growth for the sake of an unconscionable acquisition premium. Chapter 10, "The Two-and-a-Half-Ton Truck," steers through these issues.

Sin 5: Preaching Vision and Values

Despite overwhelming evidence that cultural differences must be addressed swiftly, many executives believe it is possible to merge cultures gradually, through contact and interaction. Ironically, social scientists of the 1950s referred to this discredited strategy as the "contagion approach"—analogous to the spread of infection.

You cannot merge two cultures by waving a banner proclaiming common vision and values. Cultural change doesn't come from newsletters, logos, screen savers, or success posters. It's not about hype, promotion, mantras, or prayers. Integrating two cultures requires integrating two idiosyncratic behavior sets. Chapter 11, "The Ultimate Scapegoat," offers a practical solution for aligning cultures.

Sin 6: Putting Turtles on Fence Posts

Managers begin jockeying for position early. Executives either attempt to take care of their own people or bend over backward to show impartiality, deploying as many of the acquired managers as possible. Rarely is there enough information to make informed decisions. The most common mistake is using selection decisions to balance horse-trading that began when the deal was struck.

These misguided attempts at recruiting democracy end up resembling a quota system that violates every proclamation management ever made about the importance of merit. The result is too many people in jobs that can be neither defended nor comprehended. An old Chinese proverb says: "If you see a turtle on a fence post, you know someone put it there." The proverb's relevance to modern-day mergers is apparent.

To make matters worse, executive turtles increase the moron ratio. As one Silicon Valley CEO put it, "First-rate people hire first-rate people, second-rate people hire third-rate people, and third-rate people hire morons." Mistakes at the top cascade down. Because role models are the soul and substance of culture, chapter 11 puts this issue into a cultural perspective.

Sin 7: Rewarding the Wrong Behaviors

Picture a casino in Las Vegas. Hundreds of gamblers stand at hundreds of slot machines, but the average person is interested in only the machine he is playing. Why? Because he has a stake in that machine. Managers are no different. The bigger their stake, the more they stretch to capture the rewards.

Meaningful progress rarely occurs in acquisitions until executive compensation is sorted out. Unfortunately, the architects of post-deal incentive plans are often preoccupied with funding formulas, eligibility criteria, delivery mechanisms, tax treatments, and administrative requirements. The plans become Rube Goldberg–like contraptions that defy logic, frustrate managers, and confuse participants. They lose sight of the real objective: to energize and focus behavior. Chapter 12, "The Blind Man's Dog," focuses on the real objective of transition incentives.

In the End

A PricewaterhouseCoopers survey of acquirers asked what they would do differently if they could start over. Eighty-nine percent of the respondents said they would have executed the transition more quickly. Perhaps the greatest sin is moving too slowly to capture the value in the deal.

There is no value in a prolonged transition.

FIVE FROGS
ON A LOG

1

Opportunity Lost
The Dealmaker's Nightmare

What a coup! Wired *magazine called it "a marriage tasked in heaven." The* Wall Street Journal *called it the "boldest technology deal in years, preempting competitors and ushering in a new era of convergence." And you're the dealmaker who pulled it off. Industry watchers called you a strategic genius. The* Financial Times *called you a visionary. Even your competitors were impressed. You didn't mind. Not a bit.*

So, congratulations, if they're in order. And that's a very big "if."

The story started well. Your aging baby, Global Computer, had seen the future and blinked. Saddled with fading technology and fierce competition, you counted up your mercifully huge cash kitty and went shopping for a brilliant young partner. Nexus Technologies was ideal, a Seattle prodigy with the hottest networking concept in the industry. Founded by Johnny Wu, a twenty-something Cantonese immigrant with a doctorate from Cal Tech, Nexus's wunderkinder were front-runners in a whole new market niche, but the cost of heading off hungry rivals had loaded them with life-threatening debt. Their recent IPO had soared for three months, enriching their investment bankers and some fast-thinking arbitrageurs, but had then inexplicably (though not to the bankers) sunk to single-digit oblivion.

So you had what Nexus coveted: quick cash and survival, albeit as a

*junior partner. They offered what you coveted: Global Computer's rein-
carnation as the sharpest blade in cutting-edge computerdom.*

*Business Week initially labeled you the "dealmaker of the quarter."
Other CEOs were generous with envy-spiced praise, and you suddenly
acquired a dozen new best friends. God knows, you earned that glow.
Inventing Global-Nexus wasn't easy. Twice you had to revise the offer,
juggling the cash and stock payment mix and massaging the executive
roles and compensation packages. The way those Seattle prima donnas
acted, you'd never know they were bleeding and desperate for your cash
transfusion and marketing savvy. Then came the board approvals, endless press briefings, employee announcements, and the pitch to Wall
Street.*

*In justifying the merger to the board, you waxed eloquent about
strategic and economic opportunity, complementary products, overlapping accounts, new market channels, reduced costs, scale economies,
and—best of all—that hot new technology in the near future.*

*But months have since drifted past—almost four, in fact—and the
truth is no longer beautiful. It's not ugly, but there's a little secret gnawing in your belly. Your heavenly marriage is not going well. It hasn't even
been consummated.*

*Three months ago, you told the world what you then firmly be-
lieved: Global-Nexus was about to become a spectacular whole far
greater than the sum of its already impressive parts. Unfortunately, you
may have hoisted expectations a bit high. Within weeks, impatient customers and anxious software developers began asking when they would
see the technology breakthroughs you promised. Analysts wondered
aloud about your earnings estimates. One business columnist printed
some vicious gossip. Competitors smelled blood. Corporate buyers were
publicly taking a wait-and-see position.*

*Back at Global's headquarters in Palo Alto, you began to hear dis-
turbing rumors about Johnny Wu's Nexus kids up there in Seattle. Lots
of preening about who was indispensable, suggesting lots of worry
about who was getting fired, whether the survivors would have to relocate, and, indeed, whether you "old guys" in Palo Alto knew what
you're doing. More and more, Johnny Wu doesn't return your calls,*

sometimes for days. His voice mailbox is invariably full; he's supposedly too frantic to glance at his E-mail. So now you clearly have a generation and communication gap as well as a geographical one.

What if some of those Nexus wizards jump ship before you even leave port? Will the new products ever be developed? How will you keep the few Nexus customers that signed on early if the people they relied on depart? And don't forget your own customers. Ravenous competitors are already soliciting them, while shamelessly courting your best people and attacking your reputation in the marketplace.

As time flits past with no real integration occurring, no leveraging of channels and customers, no technology transfer, no new breakthroughs, and no cost savings captured, uncertainty begins to skyrocket. It breeds anxiety and backbiting. Your new two-company sales team is united only in blaming Hart-Scott-Rodino, the entire legal profession, and Congress for stopping them from sharing data essential to pursuing new customers. When they're not ranting and raving, they're attacking one another, engineering, and product management.

How will you ever bridge the cultural gap? Suits versus T-shirts. Design review meetings versus food fights. Planning retreats versus white-water rafting trips. Even your corporate colors don't fit—teal and kelly green?

Everyone is leaning on your information systems people for customer, product, and market data. They say they have other priorities. If you step in and order them to switch priorities, what other projects will you obstruct?

So far, the critics—internal and external—have monopolized the conversation. Unencumbered by facts and gripped by paranoia, they've been describing the deal's downside to anyone who will listen. How do you quiet these naysayers? How do you prove to your customers, employees, shareholders, suppliers, vendors, and the communities in which you operate that the deal is good for them? And what about those acerbic analysts? How do you convince them you won't become yet another merger casualty?

Whom can you trust to help you deploy the new company's key people? You were sure three months ago, but now there's a different ques-

The lords of infrastructure are busily trying to dictate the pace of the transition. You've seen the list of post-deal tasks they've assembled. It isn't pretty. Twenty-six typed, single-spaced pages backed up by eighteen linear feet of Gantt charts—and not a revenue driver to be found.

tion—who will be left to deploy? With astonishing boldness, the headhunters have swooped down on the best and the brightest, most of whom can't bear delay and uncertainty. They like money, but they adore brain chic and revenge-of-the-nerds glory. They're not content with shaping the future. They want to own it.

Accordingly, star players are flocking elsewhere, and despite all those confidentiality agreements, proprietary information is seeping out to competitors. Not surprisingly, deadlines and productivity are slipping. Suddenly you're paying too many people retention fees on top of paying others severance. Overtime and rework costs are rising. So is the unplanned cost of training new people to replace the deserters. Margins are falling. Certain journalists are happy. They like self-fulfilling prophecies.

Questions are propagating faster than answers, and everyone is running out of patience. You know that the agitation over prolonged uncertainty may well abort Global-Nexus, but you don't know quite how to fix it. How do you stabilize the new organization? How do you create clarity, focus, and urgency? What do you say to whom, and when do you say it? Everybody has questions. Nobody has answers.

The lords of infrastructure are busily trying to dictate the pace of the transition. You've seen the list of post-deal tasks they've assembled. It isn't pretty. Twenty-six typed, single-spaced pages backed up by eighteen linear feet of Gantt charts—and not a revenue driver to be found.

At last sighting, your two human resource chiefs were holed up and building the mother of all compensation programs. You just wanted some guidelines for paying people. The last time you peeked in, they were debating which sabbatical program was the best. You didn't even know that Global had a sabbatical program!

Everybody wants to be involved in the transition, to control it and bend it around their own agenda. How do you get them to see this from *the perspective of the total company and keep them engaged without sacrificing progress?*

You feel overwhelmed: so much to do, so little time. So much time wasted, so little accomplished. You don't have a plan for day one, and like playing the quarterback in a kids' game of touch football, you now find that your entire team has gone out for a pass, leaving you to be sacked. Value is eroding every day. You feel your chest tightening. You know Global-Nexus is a terrific concept, a win-win deal for you and Johnny Wu and hundreds of other people, not to mention all those customers and shareholders who stand to benefit. But the merger is stalled, refuses to budge. Will it ever move forward?

Global-Nexus is slipping through your fingers.

■ ■ ■

No more champagne. No more euphoria.

Your eyes ache, your head pounds. . . . It's 3:56 A.M., and the deal-maker of the quarter keeps twisting instead of sleeping.

Some nights you wish God would postpone dawn.

Just delete it.

2

The Ugly Truth

Deciding Is Easy, Executing Is Hard

A sardonic newspaperman once said, "In war, the first casualty is truth." When it comes to corporate change and transition, the first casualty is usually shareholder value.

Companies throughout the world move from fad to fad and failure to failure in the quest for profitable growth. Each year billions of dollars are spent in the push for competitive superiority. The single greatest push for business advantage is in the area of mergers and acquisitions.

By and large, the track record is abysmal. An exhaustive analysis of hundreds of deals made in the first half of the 1990s led *Business Week* to conclude that even those deals that were several years old hadn't begun to work. Of 150 deals valued at $500 million each or more, about half actually destroyed shareholder value. Another third contributed only marginal improvements.

The statistics for the past twenty years have not favored mergers and acquisitions. Committed dealmakers insist the evidence is circumstantial. But, as Thoreau once said, "Some circumstantial evidence is very strong, as when you find a trout in the milk."

Even the technology sector is

> **There are more fools among buyers than among sellers.**
>
> *French proverb*

not immune. Nearly 40 percent of the semiconductor industry deals done in the mid-1980s actually hurt the combined revenue potential of the companies involved. A little over half of the acquisitions had no discernible effect on the combined companies' revenue potential, and a mere eight percent showed positive results.

In 1996 PricewaterhouseCoopers conducted a nationwide study of 124 recently merged or acquired companies, and found that the objec-

---

How Do They Get Away with It?

They reinvent history. Take a look at a company's annual report a few years after a disappointing acquisition. The reason for doing the original deal has been adjusted, the targets have been restated to better fit the actual results, the vagaries of the market are cited, and the litany of turmoil in the industry is chanted. Copywriters turn this stuff out faster than George Orwell's Ministry of Truth could rewrite history.

There is an old story of a medieval king who wanted, more than anything, to be a great archer. He practiced every day and carefully observed the finest archers in contests of skill. Then one day, while riding in the countryside, he passed a barn that had a dozen arrows firmly planted in a dozen bull's-eyes. He was stunned by this feat and ordered his soldiers to find the archer. They returned with a young, barefoot boy.

The king showered the boy with compliments and asked him how he managed to be so expert an archer. Embarrassed and shy, the boy glanced up at the king and said, "It's really quite simple. I notch an arrow in the bow, draw it back, aim, and release. Then I walk over to the barn and draw the bull's-eye around the arrow."

This is a form of archery frequently practiced by some of the world's most prolific dealmakers. As Malcolm Forbes once noted, "Anyone who says businessmen deal in facts, not fiction, has never read old five-year projections."

tives that drove the deal were met only half the time and often took years to be realized. Further, the least-achieved objectives had often been the most sought after, such as reductions in manufacturing costs, distribution costs, and operating expenses.

Despite this, CEO after CEO continues to buy companies, playing the odds with shareholders' cash. It reminds you of the Mad Hatter in *Alice in Wonderland*. At a tea party nicely laid out with china, linen, and silver, he took a seat, made a thorough mess on the tablecloth in front of him, moved to the next place, made a mess there, and continued around the table. In some companies this type of behavior apparently passes for acquisition strategy.

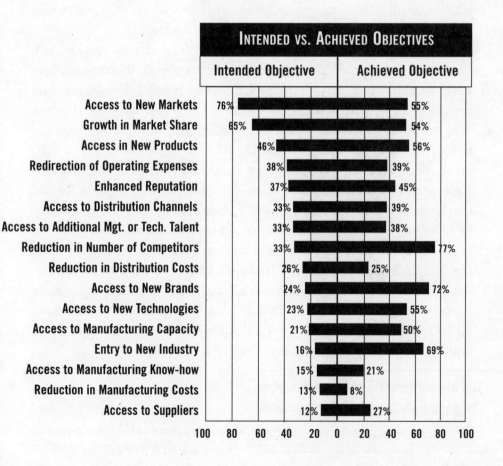

	Intended Objective	Achieved Objective
INTENDED VS. ACHIEVED OBJECTIVES		
Access to New Markets	76%	55%
Growth in Market Share	65%	54%
Access in New Products	46%	56%
Redirection of Operating Expenses	38%	39%
Enhanced Reputation	37%	45%
Access to Distribution Channels	33%	39%
Access to Additional Mgt. or Tech. Talent	33%	38%
Reduction in Number of Competitors	33%	77%
Reduction in Distribution Costs	26%	25%
Access to New Brands	24%	72%
Access to New Technologies	23%	55%
Access to Manufacturing Capacity	21%	50%
Entry to New Industry	16%	69%
Access to Manufacturing Know-how	15%	21%
Reduction in Manufacturing Costs	13%	8%
Access to Suppliers	12%	27%

100 80 60 40 20 0 20 40 60 80 100

So Why Do They Do It?

Short answer: rapid growth.

At the beginning it all sounds good—a strategic merger that lever-ages the best of two companies and promises new growth and opportu-nity. Or the acquisition of a new technology that is likely to produce breakthrough performance; a global joint venture that opens a world-wide market niche; a bold repositioning of the business in new markets. The adrenaline rush, the seductive lure of competitive advantage, the sweet scent of money, and the roar of the Wall Street crowd. After all, disasters happen to other companies.

Flush with confidence from signing a deal, fortified against critics with glowing press releases, and ready to rumble, the executive team charges headfirst into the transition minefield—with no map, no armor, and no clue. The pyrotechnics that follow are spectacular.

This phenomenon is not limited to mergers and acquisitions. Any large-scale change can drive up the adrenaline quotient. New campaigns have a seductive quality that few CEOs can resist. Like old generals searching for new battlefields, new victories, and new territory, they are on a relentless search for advantage, whether in quality, service, innova-tion, efficiency, fast-cycle or just-in-time performance—good words, great concepts. Each new campaign is infused with the hype and reli-gious fervor of a crusade. Each new skirmish is another battle for the corporate holy grail—a new cache of shareholder value. Barbarians must be killed or converted to make the world safe for the true believers.

It always sounds simple to high-level strategists. It feels as if you've cracked the code. All you have to do is execute—integrate the compa-nies, consolidate overhead units, resolve channel conflicts, reengineer support functions, transfer technologies, rationalize R&D. But at lower altitudes the execution is often a black hole of distraction, disruption, and chaos. The words come easy. The rewards do not.

The executive team charges headfirst into the transitional minefield—with no map, no armor, and no clue.

It's all an illusion. Executives everywhere, but most particu-larly those in the world's largest corporations and institutions, have a knack for falling prey to their own hype and promotion. They seem to believe it is enough to trumpet their decision loudly, promote the value proposition convincingly, and exhort the workforce to "trust" that any inconvenience or uncertainty will be short-lived and im-

> **Egos are taking precedence over future strategies.**
>
> *Sean Lance, former COO, Glaxo Wellcome, on the spate of pharmaceutical company mergers and acquisitions* (Fortune, *March 1998*)

material in the great scheme of things. Implementation is simply a detail and shareholder value is around the corner. This is quite simply delusional thinking.

This delusional state is most pronounced in high-flying industry sectors, like computer software and telecommunications, where rapid growth, sheer size, and momentum have masked strategic fumbles and where chest-beating has been elevated

> **Before employees have grasped the relationship between yesterday's panacea and today's antidote, management is already sampling tomorrow's cure-all.**

to an art form. After one such consumer products company executed a merger that doubled its size, it spent the next several months planning a communications campaign that touted some of the great partnerships— Batman and Robin, Fred Astaire and Ginger Rogers—while its market share eroded at double-digit rates and key executives defected. Transition plans, timely integration, and, apparently, customers were afterthoughts.

This behavior is also evident in bureaucratic organizations where tradition, process, and style substitute for thinking and understanding. It is especially apparent in companies with contracting markets where getting the next idea or identifying the next trend becomes more urgent than acting on it. Before employees have grasped the relationship between yesterday's panacea and today's antidote, management is already sampling tomorrow's cure-all. Implementation becomes a detail lost in hype and left to overworked, underinvested transition teams and steering committees.

Ego, Overconfidence, and Arrogance

Of course, ego plays a role in all this. When it comes to M&A, it's remarkable how much money and time is spent and how much commitment a CEO makes to buy a company and how little is spent to make it work. Frequently more cash goes to goodwill than to human resource, market, and product development.

The value proposition used to justify the wisdom of the deal is too often lost in the black hole of debt service, the uncertainty of post-deal inertia, the cold reality of hot forecasts, the struggling of overworked managers, a mind-numbing focus on cost reduction, and a short-sighted failure to invest in business growth.

The value proposition used to justify the wisdom of the deal is too often lost in the black hole of debt service, the uncertainty of post-deal inertia, the cold reality of hot forecasts, the struggling of overworked managers, a mind-numbing focus on cost reduction, and a short-sighted failure to invest in business growth. These are just a few reasons that so many mergers fail, so many joint ventures perform below expectations, and so many corporate change programs are disappointing.

Many executives take the position that executing successful transitions is merely a matter of working harder or working smarter. This position is more indicative of arrogant posturing than of a firm grip on reality. It is the simple-minded myopia of swaggering hip-shooters—no more than a seductive mirage in a wasteland of macho hype. It lures the overconfident dealmaker and the naïve savant who, blinded by occasional victories and flush from the current conquest, ignore the profusion of post-deal flops and regard failure as something that happens to other people's companies.

It's always fascinating to watch a CEO pound on the managers of an acquired company or a new product line for missing targets and then, in the next breath, browbeat them into raising their forecast. Generally they're simply cranking up the business assumptions (forecasts) to make marginal deal economics work. In some cases much of the real value gets squandered while they manipulate forecasts and budgets to justify their strategy instead of getting on with implementation. As John Kenneth

Galbraith once suggested, "Faced with having to change their views or prove there is no need to do so, most people get busy on the proof."

There is nothing wrong per se with working harder and working smarter—though the former happens more often than the latter, and more frequently among the rank and file than the senior executives. The rhetoric of "harder and smarter" wears thin when the Hawthorne Effect (performance temporarily improving with the introduction of something new) wears off. Ask any executive who has ever been enticed by a quick fix but discovered it was only a temporary work-around masquerading as a real answer.

Yet quick-fix, "working smarter" fads continue to captivate shallow tacticians who believe that articulating competitive advantage is the same as capturing it. Unfortunately, these people have forgotten or never learned the Law of Unintended Consequences—that organizational actions tend to have secondary and tertiary effects that undermine the original intent. As a disillusioned CEO once said, "Simple solutions exist only in the minds of cowboys, fools, and investment bankers." Be careful where you place your trust.

> **Chasing the holy grail of simple solutions at an unhurried pace is a fool's errand, better suited to medieval monasteries than modern businesses.**

H. L. Mencken once sagely pointed out that for every problem there is a solution that is neat, simple, and . . . wrong. There are no simple solutions in times of change because change isn't simple. There are too many moving parts. What begins as a strategic proposition evolves into a financial transaction and becomes a complex human proposition.

Transitions in today's successful company require an acute appreciation of corporate complexity backed by multidimensional plans and an ability to move quickly. Chasing the holy grail of simple solutions at an unhurried pace is a fool's errand, better suited to medieval monasteries than modern businesses.

3

More Ugly Truth
Why Performance Deteriorates

Significant acquisitions and large-scale change programs carry extraordinary opportunity costs by disrupting business, distracting employees, and diminishing current performance. Most CEOs know and understand this—at least at some conceptual level. Agreements made in the heat of a deal, however, generally blur this perspective. Moreover, change-makers consistently forget to factor it into the reengineering, total quality, or other change implementation equation.

By and large most acquisitions, joint ventures, or large-scale change efforts are driven by competition—markets, customers, products, services, and competitors. Companies usually buy other companies or launch expensive, infrastructure development programs in pursuit of some competitive advantage, some added value envisioned as an answered prayer or a cunning market maneuver. But after the announcement is made, management typically awakens to the cold reality that strategy and execution are two different animals.

Nowhere is this more apparent than in mergers and acquisitions. The high-priced bankers and lawyers exit with the close,

> **After the announcement is made, management typically awakens to the cold reality that strategy and execution are two different animals.**

leaving management to confront the challenge of producing results that justify the price, the added risk, and/or the significant disruption to current operations. To complicate matters, they face what amounts to a new company and a set of unexpected demands that can easily divert them from capturing the value that drove the deal.

Personalities and politics immediately soak up time and attention. Everybody is suddenly overwhelmed by trying to stuff two disparate corporate cultures, with two paranoid staffs and conflicting practices, into one new company that needs but one culture and far fewer employees. On the very first morning senior executives find themselves egregiously distracted by all the schmoozing, placating, and succoring that everyone not already protected by a contract seems to require.

The sentiment on the popular bumper sticker bemoaning that "it's hard to remember your goal is to drain the swamp when you're up to your posterior in alligators" is apt here. New brushfires ignite daily, and unanticipated challenges roar from around corners before the latest insurrection can be put to bed. Within days distraction becomes derailment. A time sink is born. Productive, value-creating activity is pushed to the sidelines while management scrambles to iron out details they never dreamed of before the deal.

Middle managers are set up as buffers and quickly get sucked into a maelstrom of events outside their control. They make decisions without information (otherwise commonly known as guessing) and make commitments without authority. In the meantime, senior management controls their own anxiety by creating the trappings of control. They request action plans from managers or transition teams who often have only an abstract notion of where the value is in the deal. The executives then control the implementers by weighing requests for capital against plans to reduce cost.

Inevitably, the drive to manage the transition morphs into an exercise in expense reduction—a nearly single-minded focus on swatting mosquitoes to save on the cost of bug repellent.

Inevitably, the drive to manage the transition morphs into an exercise in expense reduction—a nearly single-minded focus on swatting mosquitoes to save on the cost of bug repellent.

It's a simple equation. Improve control and manage your anxiety by holding new value creation hostage to cost-cutting. Sacrifice new revenue opportunities at the church of quick, onetime gains—where supplicants are promised a heaven filled with happy Wall Street analysts, though at the hellish expense of momentum and growth.

It's not that there is no value in cost-cutting. In consolidating industries and contracting or saturated commodity-based markets, expense reduction is a primary value driver. It allows you to lower prices and/or better manage your margins. Acquiring a competitor with an established name and customer base can reduce competition and may indeed produce scale and lower cost of sales. But unless being the low-cost producer is the limit of your strategic imagination, and unless you're willing to live on razor-thin margins, flogging it out in the trenches against "me too" competitors, there usually are better, more sustainable, and more stimulating ways to increase shareholder value.

Many managers were over-exposed in impressionable childhood years to the story in which the imprisoned, enchanted prince is released from the toad's body by a kiss from the beautiful princess. Consequently, they are certain that the managerial kiss will do wonders for the profitability of the target company. Such optimism is essential. Absent that rosy view, why else should the shareholders of company A want to own an interest in B at a takeover cost that is two times the market price they'd pay if they made direct purchases on their own? In other words, investors can always buy toads at the going price for toads. If investors instead bankroll princesses who wish to pay double for the right to kiss the toad, those kisses better pack some real dynamite. We've observed many kisses, but very few miracles. Nevertheless, many managerial princesses remain supremely confident about the future potency of their kisses, even after their backyards are knee-deep in unresponsive toads.

Warren Buffett, Berkshire Hathaway annual report (1981)

Does this sound like pessimism? Do you know the definition of a pessimist? A pessimist is an optimist who has caught up with the facts. The facts are these: In most deals and in most major change efforts, notions of profitable growth and shareholder value are quickly smothered or at least sidelined by a tidal wave of unanticipated events that drive down performance, prolong the post-deal transition, and reduce potential shareholder value creation.

How does it happen so fast? It begins with the initial announcement of a deal or a significant program of corporate change.

The Holding Pattern

Karl Weick, a noted organizational theorist, relates the following story. On October 7, 1980, on a clear, sunny morning at Atlanta's Hartsfield Airport between 8:14 A.M. and 8:20 A.M., an air traffic controller suddenly, inexplicably, put five aircraft into a holding pattern above the airport. There were ten near misses in six minutes. The control tower was enveloped in chaos as everyone scrambled to sort out the situation. Within minutes FAA investigators were sharpening pencils for the long inquiry ahead. Cool heads and experience prevailed, and all the planes landed safely. But the post-event scrutiny was probably hell.

A similar scenario unfolds with mergers, acquisitions, and many change programs, such as turning around an underperforming unit, repositioning in a new market, or reengineering a division. An initial announcement is made, and the company is promptly put into a holding pattern.

Let's take a closer look at how this works in a merger or acquisition. The deal is announced with great fanfare and optimism. Competitive advantage and new business opportunity are confidently forecast, as if just saying it makes it so. Increased shareholder value is promised, and the expectation of increased dividends and share price is proclaimed. The objective: get the investors and analysts behind it. Get the employees supportive and excited.

But wait. Don't get too excited. If the deal is of any significant size and market impact, or requires any substantial amount of ongoing investment, there is usually more to do—additional due diligence to be completed, Hart-Scott-Rodino and perhaps other regulatory reviews to get through, shareholder votes to be garnered, and so on.

So what is usually the tone of the next communication to employees? Keep cool. Don't do anything that might mess up the deal. Don't call your counterparts. Don't discuss it with customers, suppliers, or the press. In fact, don't do anything. Act as though nothing has changed. It's business as usual.

But not quite. Open positions are not filled, to leave opportunities for employees in the other company. New or ongoing infrastructure projects are put on hold, subject to review of joint system needs. Financial investments are postponed, subject to review of the other company's capital requirements and product and service development needs. Implementation of current business strategy may be slowed to avoid backtracking amid the inevitable post-deal refocusing. The company is now effectively running in place. Maintenance mode is engaged, and competitors get a free throw of the dice.

Middle management and employee frustration begins to run high. They've invested time, effort, and part of themselves in the present business. Now the plans, commitments, and expectations are disrupted. There is a sense of treading water. Uncertainty prevails because there are more questions than answers.

> **Every deal has critics, and this is their moment. The organization will never be more receptive to their warnings. While management is silent, the critics speak out, decrying the current and anticipated future state of things.**

Executives, however, are doing little more than repeating the initial hype. They, too, are treading water until the close of the deal.

Into the vacuum step the critics. Every deal has critics, and this is their moment. The organization will never be more receptive to their warnings. While management is silent, the critics speak out, decrying the current and anticipated future state of things. They are zealous and articulate. They are often opinion leaders who give voice to employee feelings and frustrations. They connect the dots and put together the pieces to construct their own dismal picture. Employees begin to listen to the wrong chorus. Speculation runs rampant. It diverts attention and drives down productivity.

While the critics sow the seeds of doubt, what do you think the competition is doing? They're having a free-for-all putting countermeasures in place. They are already calling your customers and telling them about the chaos that can be expected in the aftermath of the deal—the likelihood of service disruptions, supply shortages, increased prices, service charges, diminished quality. Not bound by the restrictions of regulatory review, they are meeting with other competitors and suppliers to discuss joint ventures and other competitive responses. They are doubling efforts to steal your prized employees and intellectual capital, both of which are vulnerable in the limbo of uncertainty.

Lost Opportunity

One aerospace company acquired a key competitor based on its investment banker's heady premise that given industry consolidation and cost synergies, the acquisition would add $6 billion to the next five years' cash flow. However, once the deal was done, the scope of the transition challenge so overwhelmed the company's leaders that they were immobilized.

After a few frustrating, indecisive meetings, some quick figuring on a piece of scrap paper revealed what $6 billion over five years actually meant. On average, the $6 billion broke down to $1.2 billion a year, $100 million a month, and $25 million a week. In a five-day business week, every business day they delayed implementing the transition strategy represented $5 million in lost opportunity.

The more time they took deciding what to do, and the longer it took them to do it, the more it would cost them in shareholder value creation opportunity.

West Side Baseball

Another danger of the holding pattern is that companies undergoing mergers or major changes in operations virtually stand still during the early months of translating the strategy that drove the decision into action. While they sort through the inevitable lists of things to do, the confusion over structural changes, the impact of shifts in individual roles, and the inescapable agony of coordinating all this with information technology, the external market and all the players are in motion.

Back in the 1950s, kids growing up on Chicago's West Side used to play a street game called West Side baseball. Like regular baseball, the game had three bases, a pitcher's mound, and a home plate. There were as many infielders and outfielders as could be found for the game. But the similarity ended there. The players used a broom-handle bat and a pink rubber ball (better known as a "pinkie"). The most important difference was the basic rule of play: after the pitcher pitched the ball, and for as long as the ball remained in the air, anybody could kick the bases anywhere they wanted.

> **If I had it to do over again, I would have done it faster.**
>
> *William Zuendt, president of Wells Fargo & Company, commenting on the company's troubled takeover of First Interstate Bancorp in 1996*

Consider the batter's dilemma. To get a hit, he has to keep his eye on the ball. However, he knows that as soon as the ball leaves the pitcher's hand, the field is in motion. First base is being kicked—maybe under a parked car. How will he know where to run? If he takes his eye off the ball to watch where first base has gone, he won't get his hit. What to do? First things first. Get the hit. And make sure your teammates have been watching the bases so you know where to run.

All large-scale change, whether merger, acquisition, process reengineering, or reorganization, sets in motion a whole new set of secondary and tertiary, temporary and permanent, intentional and unintentional changes in people, relationships, practices, procedures, and behaviors. It exerts a whole new set of external competitive and internal political pressures. It diverts managers and distracts employees.

Following the announcement of a merger or an acquisition, companies are virtually standing still while the playing field is in motion. If they take their eyes off the ball and lose track of priorities, that base hit will be a long time coming and a home run will be impossible.

Speed Makes a Difference

The plain fact is that implementation is everything. Words must be translated into action, action into early wins, and early wins into profitable growth. Yes, *early* wins. In a technology-driven, globally competitive environment where the speed of information transfer, and thus competitive intelligence, is measured in nanoseconds, if you're not implementing at the speed of light, your opportunities will dissolve before you can extract the rewards.

This was reinforced in the 1996 PricewaterhouseCoopers mergers and acquisitions survey that found that the speed of transition clearly made a difference. Companies that reported accelerating the transition after the deal also reported achieving over 80 percent of their objectives on a timely basis. Moreover, the accelerated transitions had a clearly favorable effect on the most meaningful performance metrics—gross margin, margin cash flow, productivity, profitability, and speed to market.

Change is expensive and delay can be catastrophic. A prolonged transition adds cost, slows growth, destroys profit, and decreases cash flow. It prolongs the pain and reduces or postpones the payback. There is no value in a prolonged transition.

The data confirm what many accept as a fact: change is expensive, and delay can be catastrophic. A prolonged transition adds cost, slows growth, destroys profit, and decreases cash flow. It prolongs the pain and reduces or postpones the payback. There is no value in a prolonged transition. When asked, "If you had it to do over again, what would you do differently?" nine out of ten participants in the PricewaterhouseCoopers survey said they would move faster during the post-deal transition.

The High Cost of Delay

Despite a clear sense of urgency, many executives do not comprehend just how expensive delay really is. For example, three banks decided to form a joint venture to consolidate and lower the cost of backroom operations. Despite the substantial economic opportunity within their grasp, the new entity was mired in constant recycling of the business plan. Finally, frustrated with senseless delays, the CEO of the venture pointed out to the board that each day they delayed the launch of the new business was costing the owners more than $200,000 in duplicated headcount and real estate and maintenance costs, which were simply driving up the cost of the venture.

In the wake of announcing a multibillion-dollar, multinational consumer products merger, the CEO of another new entity refused to communicate anything beyond the announcement until the deal was closed for fear that it might damage performance. Within one month both companies experienced substantial erosion in productivity and profitability anyway.

When casting about for an answer to this precipitous drop, they discovered that the lack of communication was leading to growing internal resentment and labor discord. The entire workforce was distracted. Error rates were up. Volume was down and reputation was at an all-time low. The cost of this failure to communicate could be calculated at millions of dollars.

These examples reinforce an important, if not obvious, point—until you can count and visualize the costs as they add up, the notion that a prolonged transition is expensive seems to be a purely theoretical concept.

How Do These Costs Accumulate?

Distraction, disruption, and uncertainty drive the economics of transition. They are rarely calculated into the business case. If they were, everyone would accelerate the transition to get past the dis-

It's Christmas if you're competing against merging companies.

ruption. The most common consequences of prolonged transitions involve market share, productivity, margins, uncertainty, downsizing, and stakeholder defections.

Market Share Shrinks

Managers who are mired in internal problems neglect external concerns. They lose sight of customers, competitors, and markets. Salespeople concerned over who controls which accounts in which territories for which products and services take their frustrations to the customers. Confused and worried employees make mistakes—orders are misplaced, taken incorrectly, or duplicated; deliveries are slow, partial, or wrong. Service deteriorates.

This creates an opportunity for competitors. They take advantage of the confusion. Often they stimulate greater customer and employee uncertainty by fabricating and spreading rumors. It's Christmas if you're competing against merging companies.

Additionally, customers noticing post-deal deterioration quickly lose patience. They object to underwriting their vendors' mistakes. When AT&T acquired NCR a few years back, the transition left delivery and third-party support unresolved. Their customers didn't wait around for service to improve. The rest is history.

Even markets considered strongholds for an acquirer will shrink if customers have other options. United Airlines' attempt to lock in passengers through vertical expansion into auto rental and hotels had a disastrous effect on market share. While it attempted to sort out its acquisitions of Hertz and Westin, American Airlines effortlessly captured share in Chicago, United's headquarters.

Before Northwest Airlines and Republic Airlines merged more than a decade ago, 85 percent of both airlines' flights departed on time. Within a month of their merger on-time performance had nose-dived to 25 percent.

One Silicon Valley chipmaker let three months pass before assuring its key customers—largely computer—makers—that its merger would not jeopardize their accounts or the timely delivery of their orders. Meanwhile, its customers, wanting to ensure against shortages, began to split their orders among rival suppliers. That three-month silence cost the chip-maker $30 million in orders for a single product line.

Notably, the customers that don't flee to other suppliers protect themselves against perceived delays or shortages by increasing their regular orders, only to cancel them later if things get back to normal.

Productivity Declines

Dealmakers spend far more energy hyping their brainchild to the outside world than providing a rationale to the people charged with carrying it out. This leaves employees with more questions than answers. Confused about today's priorities and tomorrow's direction, anxious employees spend inordinate amounts of time speculating with peers about the murky future. Mistakes are made. Calls to the customer service department climb. Productivity sags, then plunges.

Before Northwest Airlines and Republic Airlines merged more than a decade ago, 85 percent of both airlines' flights departed on time. Within a month of their merger on-time performance had nose-dived to 25 percent. Most business travelers would argue that little has improved at the airline since then.

Margins Narrow

As productivity drops, labor costs climb. Distracted employees serve customers badly, take longer to complete tasks, and make mistakes. These mistakes have to be corrected, driving rework and supply costs up and reducing the productivity of other employees. Making matters worse, many of these employees hide their mistakes for fear of losing their jobs. This has a domino effect, reducing the productivity of others and driving down company performance.

Anxious employees also hoard supplies, afraid of cutbacks under the new regime. One executive was mystified when twelve gross of self-stick notes vanished from an office supply cabinet. They turned up hidden behind the desk of a worried secretary who wanted them "just in case." Less amusing are the hoarders of more vital items in short supply—such as electronic components that other workers need for their daily output.

Such squirreling away creates unexpected scarcities that boost supply costs and erode margins.

> Competitors see the post-announcement uncertainty as an opportunity to lure anxious employees to greener (and more stable) pastures. This is especially true for professionals in jobs for which there is greater demand than supply. As soon as a merger, acquisition, or major restructuring is announced, competitors send in their best recruiters with premium offers, sign-up bonuses, and special incentives for referrals.
>
> Some companies set up temporary recruiting offices down the street from an acquired or downsizing company. In out-of-state situations, the true predators establish remote offices to allow new recruits to telecommute without having to relocate.

Uncertainty Ignites an Exodus

Good people thrive under managers who lead with clarity, decisiveness, and panache. When the post-deal environment becomes an ocean of uncertainty, or when the latest change initiative fosters another round of groans, the first to get out are the company's best and brightest. These key contributors see no reason to put their own careers on hold while their leaders tread water.

Where do they go? Dry land—the competition—with their heads full of proprietary information, customer connections, and industry relationships. They leave behind stalled projects, worried customers, frantic colleagues, and a daunting learning curve for those trying to take their place.

Certain employees, notably salespeople, are known for jumping ship early while their knowledge is in demand and they can sell effectively against their former company. Their value to competing companies is high, and the return on recruiting them is captured immediately. These relocated employees strike quickly and do serious damage to their former employers.

Knee-jerk Downsizing Incurs Higher Costs

How can it be that in this age of information some executives are surprised to learn that there is a clear and direct correlation between employee morale, productivity, and customer satisfaction?

How can it be that in this age of information some executives are surprised to learn that there is a clear and direct correlation between employee morale, productivity, and customer satisfaction?

When the conversion of systems and the transfer of information and responsibilities take longer than expected (as they usually do); when the costs are more than planned (as they usually are); when revenue opportunities play second fiddle to cost-cutting (as they usually do); and when the company faces disappointing post-deal performance (as it usually does), executives often react by slashing even more off the payroll.

Most companies do this with consummate ineptness. Managers are given headcount targets or human resource cost targets and told to cut. The cutting is done generally without regard to growth strategy or impact on key operating practices. Worst of all, across-the-board cuts generally are applied equally to profitable and unprofitable units, damaging the performance of the profitable groups.

Overlooked is the fact that companies staff to the requirements of their current systems and practices. When heads are cut without changing the processes those heads support, there will be an additional burden on the remaining employees. Systems break down. Things fall through the cracks, and time and attention are diverted from generating revenue to fighting fires. Severance costs, lawsuits, early retirement programs, bad publicity, back-fill recruiting costs, business disruptions, customer turnover—all contribute to a net loss rather than a net gain.

Though not all companies are advocates of a slash-and-burn philosophy, there is no clean way to downsize and come out looking like a responsible corporate citizen. The downsizing company looks and smells like a company that is struggling and retrenching, not like a winner that you would want to patronize.

To complicate matters further, employees who know their tenure is limited to a post-deal transition period while systems and practices are converted and handed off are singularly unmotivated in customer service, receivables collection, project completion, and record-keeping. They are understandably more focused on finding new jobs than executing current tasks. In fact, they can quickly become loose cannons if meaningful retention and transition performance incentives are not in place.

Many companies find out too late that they have cut too deeply to complete the post-deal transition on a timely basis or to support the growth objectives at the heart of their strategy. As a result, they often are faced with a need to resume hiring. Some of the new hires may require expensive, time-consuming training. Others may be former employees who are rehired at a premium to their old salary or are given lucrative consulting or contracting work in addition to the early retirement payouts that may have cost the company so dearly.

Though not all companies are advocates of a slash-and-burn philosophy, there is no clean way to downsize and come out looking like a responsible corporate citizen. The downsizing company looks and smells like a company that is struggling and retrenching, not like a winner that you would want to patronize. All transitions should be about growing, not about cutting. You cannot shrink your way to prosperity.

The most important resource for most companies is human capital—the knowledge embedded in the minds of the employees. "Re-sizing" or "right-sizing" a company should emphasize reallocation of resources to drive growth, not simply cutting expenses. Otherwise, it's just "dumb-sizing."

Delays Lead to Stakeholder Defections

Next to customers, employees and investors represent two other very important stakeholder groups. In a transition, employees will tolerate a certain amount of delay. But these same employees rapidly lose confidence in management that fails to take early, firm stands and set a clear direction. Their natural self-interest makes it difficult for them to support a tentative transition or respect an equivocal leader. This often results in increased turnover of the people a company can least afford to lose.

Investors and analysts have no more patience than employees. Wall

Street gives a newly merged company about one fiscal quarter to get its act together. If the company has made no apparent progress toward the deal's objectives after three months, analysts begin losing confidence, prompting a rush of "sell" or "hold" versus "buy" recommendations.

> **Other people's "best practices" work best in other people's companies. Best practices are based on past conditions. The new conditions wrought by a merger often cry out for a fresh point of view.**

Misrepresenting the Deal as a "Merger of Equals"

Among the pervasive delusions of dealmakers is the assumption that two disparate corporate cultures can combine the "best practices of each" and achieve what optimists call "a merger of equals." One of the more unfortunate fads in recent years has been the tendency of acquirers to announce a merger of equals in which the plan is to select the best practices from each organization. Usually this is an accommodation to the acquired company's CEO—sometimes as a condition of the deal to stroke his or her ego and sometimes as a misguided attempt to allay employee fears about whether they will be valued.

A CEO's announcement of a merger of equals creates an expectation that the two sides must agree on best practices. This gives managers throughout the combined organization an explicit license to engage in an interminable debate over who has the best practices. This competition retards integration, builds resentment, fosters disappointment, drives down productivity, and slows the capture of new business opportunities.

Other people's "best practices" work best in other people's companies. Best practices are based on past conditions. The new conditions wrought by a merger often cry out for a fresh point of view.

> **Casey Stengel, the renowned former New York Yankees coach, once said, "Getting good players is easy. The hard part is getting them to play together." Imagine a professional ball team on which every player could debate the signals and challenge game strategy. This is but one of the challenges in a merger of equals.**

Out of sheer frustration, many CEOs are driven to publicly reposition the "merger of equals" as an acquisition to regain control and perspective on who bought the right to make these decisions. Even true mergers, in which there is simply a pooling between companies of roughly similar size and capability, tend to be driven by a strategic complementarity that suggests that one side is superior to the other in certain capabilities, if not certain markets, products, or services.

There is no such thing as a merger of equals. One side always dominates, usually the side with the greater size or stronger, more aggressive management. Given this, it should not be surprising that more than half of all senior executives in acquired companies leave voluntarily within the first three years.

A CEO's announcement of a merger of equals gives managers throughout the combined organization an explicit license to engage in an interminable debate over who has the best practices. This competition retards integration, builds resentment, fosters disappointment, drives down productivity, and slows the capture of new business opportunities.

Those executives who remain are often torn between angrily defending their preacquisition practices as superior and succumbing to a kind of malicious obedience that takes pleasure in carrying out the new boss's obvious follies and refraining from saving him from himself. You need only observe a few of these emotional games to conclude that the only thing more corrupting than power is powerlessness.

4

The Law of the Band-Aid

The Need for Accelerated Transition

Eliminating the Pain

Post-deal setbacks and the attendant distraction and disruption of a transition are fertile ground for Murphy's Law. The problems are predictable. The only difference from transition to transition is in the degree of severity. The real question is, why would anyone want to prolong it? Short of a neurotic need for abuse, there is no compelling reason to prolong a transition once the change has been announced or the deal has been closed.

Remember your first few cuts and scrapes as a kid? Worse than the initial injury was the dreaded Band-Aid removal—that slow, hair-pulling, torturous peel. Ouch! It didn't take long to learn that one quick rip works best. The same holds true for corporate transitions. There is no value in prolonging the pain or delaying the inevitable. In fact, it invariably makes things worse.

From a purely financial standpoint, the faster you complete the transition, the faster you realize returns on your investment. From a competitive standpoint, speed allows you to exploit post-deal opportunities on your own

> **Cleverness has never been associated with long delays.**
>
> *Sun-tzu,* The Art of War, *circa 500 B.C.*

terms, forcing competitors to react and denying them the luxury of a calculated response. Speed provides room to maneuver and the ability to
surprise. From a personal standpoint, speed reduces pain. It decreases
the amount of time that you are forced to deal with the crippling effects
of uncertainty.

Prolonged indecision and delayed results foster impatience and sow
seeds of doubt throughout the company. As unfair as it may seem, the
limits of tolerance are very short. Once the deal closes, Wall Street gives
you one fiscal quarter to show meaningful progress against merger objectives before questioning the competency of the management team.
Employee patience and capacity for uncertainty are equally limited. If
your transition is not progressing along a hundred-day critical path, you
are behind the power curve. Performance and the capture of new opportunity are being suboptimized.

Bridgestone, the Japanese tire-maker, bought Firestone in the
late 1980s. Hoping not to disrupt Firestone's operations, the parent company proceeded deliberately and gradually to integrate the
two manufacturers, but the snail's pace was disconcerting to many
Firestone employees and managers.

As an essayist in the *Economist* observed, "The velvet glove approach was a mistake." When a takeover takes place, employees
expect dramatic changes and are prepared to accept them. By acting too slowly, Bridgestone lost the chance to make big changes
and worsened the culture clash between American and Japanese
methods.

This understanding of time limits would seem to be intuitive, but
some people never see the light. They only feel the heat. Describing
their approach in empty expressions such as "letting the dust settle" or
"getting the lay of the land," they attempt to justify delayed action.
Later they find themselves reacting to events that might have been pre-
vented.

Novell Corporation learned this lesson the hard way in the acquisition of the applications group that created WordPerfect Suite. Delays in key investment, development, and sales and marketing decisions, followed by knee-jerk responses to declining post-deal performance, led to substantially diminished share-

> **The start-up period was too slow, production costs were too high, and Harsco failed to gain market penetration.**
>
> *Derek Hathaway, chairman of Harsco, after charging off $8 million when the company closed a small truck plant it had acquired only a few years earlier for $2 million*

holder value and a reevaluation of corporate strategy. Disaster. Eighteen months after the purchase, the applications group was sold for $124 million—down from the original purchase price of $1.4 billion.

In his classic book *The Art of War*, the Chinese general Sun-tzu twenty-five centuries ago wrote, "Cleverness has never been associated with long delays." He was, of course, referring to fighting a war. Nevertheless, the lesson applies here.

Just as there is a time value to money, there is a time value to employee and investor enthusiasm. The earlier you stimulate that enthusiasm, the sooner you can leverage that support into real momentum. People like winners. And they like to sign on to winning teams. Early post-deal wins and clear evidence of early momentum translate into early enthusiasm.

Your Brain on Speed

The longer it takes to reduce ambiguity and position the company for growth, the greater the likelihood of diminished employee support, increased confusion, extensive alienation, and widespread resistance. There is even a neurological basis for this reaction. The brain learns by perceiving patterns. When things are happening slowly—incrementally—the patterns are difficult to perceive. The brain cannot connect the dots and form a coherent picture of where things are going.

Think about it for a moment. If you watched a film at the rate of one frame per day for the next several months, do you think you would ever

---

**If the complex deals of the 1980s
taught us anything, it's that making an
acquisition work demands complete
management attention to integrating
the two businesses. The quicker
that's accomplished, the better.**

Business Week, *January 15, 1990*

---

figure out the plot? Not likely.

The same thing happens in slow-moving transitions. Because the employees never quite get it, they develop extraordinary levels of uncertainty and anxiety. Anxiety is painful. When a prolonged transition extends the anxiety, resentment builds. If you want the post-deal transition to be infused with clarity instead of confusion, with enthusiasm instead of alienation, you must build speed and momentum.

The Myth of Resistance to Change

Speed also reduces resistance. It's remarkable how many executives have been duped by the notion that people resist change and that a slow transition gives employees time to adjust. Wrong! People do not resist change per se—that is a myth. If it were a fact that people resist change, no progress would ever be made anywhere. Revolutions would not take place. Innovation would be nonexistent. Obviously, someone is driving change.

What people resist is punishment. And the single most punishing effect of change is uncertainty. Prolonged uncertainty is unbearable. The longer a transition is dragged out, the more it punishes all employees and alienates a company's best and brightest, the very people needed to make the new arrangement work. To reduce the resistance, you must reduce punishment.

In medieval times, when map-makers ran out of known world before they ran out of parchment, they wrote in the legend, "Here be dragons." It was a clear and unambiguous warning to back off. The notion of employee resistance to change is the modern-day equivalent of that warning, and no more meaningful.

This concept is not rocket science. It should be accessible to anyone who gives it a little thought and is not emotionally tone-deaf to the impact of prolonged uncertainty. You don't win support for change by dragging it on indefinitely.

During transitions, economic value is, in large part, a function of speed. Companies that successfully navigate change learn faster, act quicker, and adapt sooner. When a decision is made to alter products, to target specific markets or business processes, or to transact a merger, implementation can be compromised quickly by competitors' countermeasures and internal politics. Successful companies compress time, stimulate competitive business focus, and drive early shareholder value.

The Wandering CEO

These lessons are generally lost on the many shortsighted executives who assume that signing a set of papers renders a deal "done" and lets them off the hook, while subordinates are left to sort out the details. Consider the following case of the CEO of a high technology company.

After engineering the purchase of a competitor in a huge deal that doubled the size of his company, he left for Europe for what he considered a "normal" three-month vacation in the sun. The crucial early moves to capture the value in the deal were left to the CEO of the acquired company—a man who was retiring and widely perceived as a lame duck—and a pack of browbeaten lieutenants who couldn't see beyond their own silos and had neither the will nor the authority to carry out critical early actions.

When the CEO finally returned, he found his company in acute disarray, reeling backward from the toxic effects of high anxiety, loss of key technologists to competitors, a raft of stalled R&D projects, and a failed plant consolidation strategy. Years later the effects linger, and the company never fully realized the values touted by the dealmakers.

"One calendar year (in transition) is equivalent to seven years of normal growth, and so you have to move at an unbelievable pace."

—*John Chambers, CEO, Cisco Systems,*
in VAR Business, *September 15, 1996*

Speed means rapidly putting the piers in place and laying down the platform for the timely capture of economic value. It is about how to launch all the critical actions in a merger, acquisition, or large-scale change in the first one hundred days, the outer limit of employee enthusiasm, customer tolerance, and Wall Street patience. It's about accelerating any transition—by maximizing the value sought as early as possible while minimizing the decline in performance that inevitably accompanies unsettling change. It's about treating change like removing a Band-Aid. No hesitation. No delay. One quick movement.

Rip. Sting. Done.

5

260 Priorities
Economic Value Creation

You've just taken on the biggest challenge of your career. You're the new skipper of one of the biggest ships in your industry's pond. More people are depending on you now than ever before. Even your proud mother, with good motherly intentions, has reminded you how far you could now fall.

As soon as your crew climbed aboard, almost half of them new to you, your anxious and expectant board of directors shoved your ship-away from the dock, wished you luck, and reminded you that you have a schedule to keep.

You wish there were time for a "shakedown" cruise—the crew clearly need it. Even before you cast off, two people fell overboard hoisting the anchor and a fight broke out below deck over who would get the biggest stateroom. Your officers want to know how you'll reach your destination on time since you're already several weeks behind schedule. The cook has too much flour and no coffee. Funny smells are coming from the engine room. No one but you seems to notice the large barge closing in just off the port bow.

You're wondering if you will even make it out of the harbor alive.

Now, if you really were a ship's skipper, you'd probably bark out orders to a trained crew who would respond immediately with maximum effort.

Unfortunately, your corporate crew includes a lot of new members who have never sailed together before, and each of them wants to steer the ship. This crew doesn't follow orders very well. They have to be *convinced* of which things they need to act on to keep your ship on course.

In a nutshell, this is the challenge facing most executives who embark on a merger, acquisition, or large-scale change: convincing managers to work together as a team and to act first on those things that drive shareholder value.

Even under normal business conditions, it's a challenge to get executives to work together as a team and to get them to concentrate corporate resources on decisive objectives. People who are bright, independent thinkers—the qualities that probably got them hired in the first place—have their own ideas about what needs to be done. These ideas often differ because, understandably, each person looks at the problems from a different perspective. Most of the time these differences aren't reconciled. When they are, the arguments are usually based on personal testimony or anecdotal facts, not on thoughtful analysis.

This dilemma is especially evident in mergers and acquisitions. Why? Most deals are done on a conceptual basis. They are motivated by high-level visions of competitive advantage that ought to be achievable—at least in the minds of the dealmakers. However, while senior executives can imagine the value ahead, they seldom perceive, much less ponder, the operational realities of getting from here to there. Conceptually clear, the solution remains operationally muddled, and the priorities are based more on anecdotes than on data.

> **People being people, I'm not at all convinced that a management team in the midst of integration will necessarily decide for the common good. Until they learn to work together, they need the integrity of a credible, systematic process.**
>
> *John Varley, Chief Executive, Retail Financial Services, Barclays PLC*

When a company enters a transition period, it encounters a whole new set of obstacles and challenges to achieving consensus on business priorities. Almost immediately, transition activities conflict with day-to-day operations, delaying progress on both. Absent a clear set of priorities, and human nature being what it is, people are more likely to carry out those actions that are easiest to accomplish and personally rewarding rather than the actions most likely to drive shareholder value and capture early returns.

So how exactly do you get a new group of smart and motivated executives to start operating like a team? How exactly do you make sure that limited resources are concentrated on actions that really do drive shareholder value? How exactly do you cut through the operational clutter and convince the executive team to act quickly on the right things?

Well, short of issuing directives and diminishing the team's sense of personal contribution and added value, a leader doesn't.

What you need is a process that allows executive team members to convince *themselves* which things need to be done. A process that gets all the key executives in the same room, at the same time, with the same data, making the same decisions about which actions will capture shareholder value.

This is *exactly* what value driver analysis is designed to do. *Value driver analysis* is a rigorous, disciplined, financially driven process that helps executive teams rapidly reach agreement on the 20 percent of the transition initiatives likely to drive 80 percent of the economic value, with the highest probability of success, in the shortest possible time frame. This analysis is typically conducted for several different time frames (for example, three, six, and twelve months) and identifies which initiatives, or value drivers, should be acted upon in each time frame. It ensures proper phasing and allocation of resources over time. Consider the following true story.

260 Priorities

"But we already know what we have to do," said the CEO of a major software company. "We have thirteen typed, single-spaced pages of priorities. Two hundred and sixty in all."

An adviser asked, "Is that in serial or alphabetical order?"

"It's by business unit and function. Don't be sarcastic."

"Sorry. So who put these two hundred and sixty items together?"

"We put together some business unit and functional transition teams."

"Were they working in isolation or working across teams?"

"Well, they were working within their own groups."

"Can we tell from this list how one team's priorities influence another team's priorities?"

"Not really. Well, actually no."

"So we have neither a sense of priority nor a sense of how these things interact with each other?"

"Well, yes, but these are all smart guys, they know how these things interact."

"Okay, so why is the transition at a full stop?"

"That's the problem. We have to run the business. This is the busiest time of the year. We don't have enough time or people. No one has enough time. They keep telling me we need a plan. But no plan ever materializes. We are paralyzed. Everybody is distracted. This transition is moving like the Mendenhall Glacier."

"Well, obviously when everything is a priority, nothing is, and it's hard to know where to start. So we should start by setting some realistic priorities."

"We know what the priorities are."

"Out of the two hundred and sixty actions, you know what the priorities are? If that's the case, why don't they just get started on them?"

"Well, not everyone agrees on what exactly the top priorities are. Or, for that matter, on whether we can afford to invest resources in all of them. I think the senior management team knows, but not everyone else agrees."

"Let's try something—a simple test. The executive team is all here. Let's see if we can at least sort out the top five priorities. Why don't you list them, and I'll write them on this chartpad."

Ten minutes later. . . .

"Those aren't the top five!" says the head of sales and marketing. *"You left out at least three critical items."*

"I completely disagree with that list," says the head of administration. *"It leaves out every one of our back-office initiatives."*

"Okay," the adviser says, *"let's add the top three back-office initiatives and the sales force automation project. Now, I think I know where this is going. Before we duplicate the entire list of two hundred and sixty actions, let's see if we can at least get agreement on the priority of these ten, okay?"*

In unison, everyone nods. The CEO says, "This should be easy."

"Okay," the adviser begins, *"start with priority number one. Will that have a greater financial impact than priority number two?"* *The tally: seven people, seven minutes, three yes votes, and four no votes.*

"Maybe that one was too difficult," says the adviser. *"How about number one versus number three?"* *Seven people, five minutes, four voting yes, two voting no, one disgusted abstention.*

"Okay," says the adviser, *"maybe the problem is with action number one. Let's compare number two with number three. Which one will have the greater financial impact?"* *Seven people, eight minutes, three yeses, two nos, and two disgusted abstentions.*

The CEO holds up both of his hands. "Okay, okay, I think we get the point. How do we fix it?"

"Well, part of the problem," responds the adviser, *"is that you are all operating with different information, making different assumptions, and drawing different conclusions. It is not surprising that you are having a difficult time agreeing. What we need is to have everyone operating off the same set of data on each action, and we need to test different assumptions in real time."*

"So all we have to do is gather the data necessary to rank the actions on financial impact?" *asked the CEO.*

"Sorry," says the adviser, *"but that's only half the equation. Not everything that has high financial impact has a high probability of success. And we want to be sure we're not wasting time and resources on something with a low probability of success. Everything should be evaluated on both financial impact and probability of success."*

"It sounds like a lot of work," counters the CEO. *"Is this really necessary? After all, each one of these actions has to get done no matter what."*

"Perhaps," the adviser responds, *"but evaluating probability of success is critical to the effective allocation of resources and timing of these*

actions. Let me give you an example. Then you can decide. Okay?"

"Okay!"

"Everyone here is enthusiastic about embedding your core technology into the acquired company's products. It was one of the primary drivers behind the acquisition. You said that this was the highest priority and that maximum financial impact could be achieved only by porting your technology to the acquired products in nine months—in time for the holiday shopping season. Your VP of engineering says it will take twelve man-years of a development team's time, and you cannot pull people off current projects, correct?"

"Correct," replies the CEO.

"Twelve man-years over nine months adds up to roughly fourteen to fifteen engineers and programmers working on this for nine months. How many of your trained technologists can you redeploy to this project?"

"Maybe one or two."

"Can you use some of the acquired company's people for this?"

"Maybe one or two."

"Sounds like you're short about eleven engineers and programmers. Do you have access to that many additional trained people?"

"No."

"Can you use contract programmers?"

"No. This is sensitive intellectual property."

"So how will you get them?"

"Not sure."

"Where will you get them?"

"Don't know."

"How long might it take to recruit as many as you need?"

"Six to eight months, if we're lucky. Probably longer."

"Help me out here. What would you say is the probability of success of delivering that application in the nine-month time frame?"

"Well, I guess pretty low."

"On a scale of one to ten, with ten being high, where would you put it?"

"To be honest with you, on that basis, it's probably a one."

"That sounds like gamblers' odds. Why waste resources and frustrate staff in the near term on such a long shot when those same resources could be allocated to something with comparable financial impact but higher probability of success? It seems you have two choices. If other projects are not as critical, pull people from there. Or make this one a relatively lower priority until you have recruited the resources to pull it off. This is why we need to balance financial impact with probability of success when establishing priorities."

It should be clear that this organization was poised to enter merger martyrdom. Despite what the CEO said, they didn't have priorities, they just had an all-encompassing list of things to do—big things, little things, everything. They didn't have consensus. They just had points of view. When they did take action, it was largely on the wrong things. Though their resources, staff, time, and capital were all finite, they failed to execute the most fundamental tactical action of all—allocating resources first to actions with predictably high payoff and success.

When setting out to implement a major transition, most companies create an encyclopedic list of everything they believe should be done and attempt to organize it all in a rational project plan. This is mistake number one. Unfortunately, everyone has a full-

> **They failed to execute the most fundamental tactical action of all—allocating resources first to actions with predictably high payoff and success.**

time day job managing the going concern. No one has the time, energy, or even the patience for the second career defined by the project plan. The sheer volume of prerequisite steps, unanticipated costs, and time-consuming minutia identified by well-meaning staffers is overwhelming. So senior management splits the tasks among transition teams. This is mistake number two.

The response of executives and middle managers on the transition teams is predictable. They have no time for this. Their attention migrates back to their day job. The transition falls through the cracks. Transition meetings are jammed in when and if there is time. Commitments to transition responsibilities become a choking anxiety and a major distraction.

As the transition slows to a crawl, the CEO expresses his empathy, rallies the troops, and exhorts the minions to double their efforts to get it all done. This is mistake number three.

The transition teams launch a renewed effort to get everything done and out of the way. This is mistake number four. By trying to do everything, they dilute their efforts and spin their wheels. Nothing is fully capitalized. Everything is suboptimized.

Analogies between business and war are common today. Most

Concentration of Resources

When the Mongols invaded China, they might have tried to scale the Great Wall and then lay siege to the entire country. However, this would have consumed their resources and left the army in a weakened state.

Genghis Khan was wise enough to take a different approach. He asked, "How can we concentrate our resources where they'll do the most good?"

"The wall ends somewhere," he reasoned. That is where he directed his troops. It took centuries for the Chinese to build the Great Wall, and it took the Mongols a few months to ride around it.

That flanking strategy seems obvious, yet many leaders ignore the lesson. The same tactic provided the Germans with an advantage in World War II. France's leading military thinkers, clearly numbed by World War I, built the Maginot Line, a series of super-fortifications that were to protect France from future German incursions. Like the Chinese, the French left their flanks open to incursion. Hitler's Panzers just blitzed around the wall, which ended at the Belgian border, and swallowed France. The Germans concentrated their resources where they would have the highest probability of success.

When alternative business decisions vie for the same pool of resources, base your priorities on those actions that promise the greatest impact with the highest probability of success.

books on business strategy reach back through twenty-five hundred years of war-fighting manuals, restating one military principle after another and applying them to business. The most enduring of these principles is the principle of concentration—putting resources to their highest and best use by concentrating them at decisive points, that is, where they will have the greatest impact with the highest probability of success. The principle of concentrating resources is the heart of value driver analysis.

As we pointed out in the first chapter, an accelerated transition is one of the best ways to avoid post-deal oblivion. An accelerated transition depends on taking rapid, meaningful *action* and concentrating resources where they will do the most good.

Value driver analysis provides the stimulus for *early, focused action*. It is a fast, objective process for sorting out the execution priorities, timing, and costs so as to build executive consensus and accelerate the capture of operational benefits and investor returns. It focuses and mobilizes the leadership team and—most important—compels them to *act*. It is not about strategy. It's about execution of strategy. It's about getting out of the harbor alive and then winning every leg of the race.

Plotting a Course

Imagine you've just received from your line managers, staff groups, consultants, lawyers, and accountants the consolidated list

> **It is not about strategy. It's about execution of strategy.**

of transition activities that must be completed "immediately": change the sales support system platform from UNIX-based to Windows NT; restructure financial reporting to support the new channel structure; close three plants in two states; eliminate one-third of the products in the catalog; restructure sales territories; eliminate overlapping accounts; renegotiate distributor contracts; sublease surplus real estate; design the new logos and letterhead; begin manufacturing the flagship product in the new offshore facility; kill three big development projects and accelerate the development of a fourth; hire two new regional sales managers and a Washington liaison; design a new sales incentive plan; select a new retirement plan record-keeper; drop off the laundry, pick up milk, feed the cat, and on and on.

You are staring at the longest to-do list you have ever seen. It is a mind-numbing, morale-destroying, ego-deflating litany of actions that makes your knees buckle—and you can already think of a dozen things that were left off!

You are staring at the longest to-do list you have ever seen. It is a mind-numbing, morale-destroying, ego-deflating litany of actions that makes your knees buckle.

If you are like most companies in transition, nearly everything becomes a priority. Why? Because the heads of each functional area, business unit, or special project focus primarily on the needs of their own organizations. They want to reduce uncertainty, stabilize their organization, eliminate the distractions, and get on with it. Moreover, they have personal biases and ambitions. This leaves you with irreconcilable demands for resources, competing interests, and conflicting priorities.

Now, imagine that instead of appearing on a long list, all these actions are arrayed on a simple matrix. Low to high financial impact on the vertical axis, and low to high probability of success on the horizontal axis.

Imagine that for each action on the list, your executives have gathered and analyzed relevant information, discussed their assumptions, and *agreed* on the relative financial impact and probability of success. They plotted their results, handed you this *single* piece of paper (see Transition and Integration Priorities figure), and said to you, in unison: "Look, boss, over the next three months we think we ought to concentrate our time, money, and attention on those things in the upper right-hand corner—the high-impact, high-probability-of-success actions. So what do you think?"

Once you regained consciousness, you would probably say that you agreed and that you wanted to know what you could do to help.

This isn't fantasy or wishful thinking. It's called value driver analysis. It is not some cold, antiseptic, backroom financial planning and analysis exercise. It's better to have reasonable estimates, or even

Transition and Integration Priorities

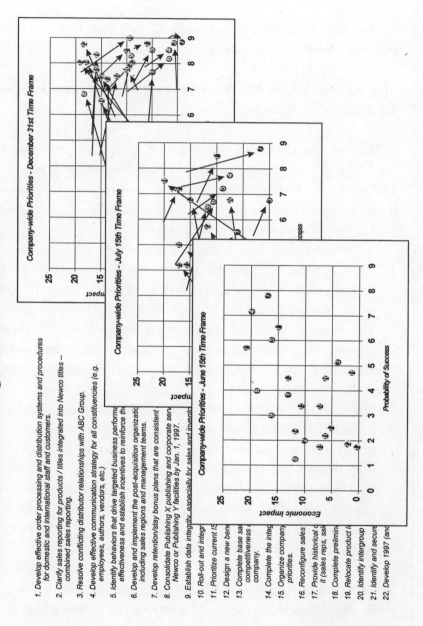

Company-wide Priorities - December 31st Time Frame

Company-wide Priorities - July 15th Time Frame

Company-wide Priorities - June 15th Time Frame

1. Develop effective order processing and distribution systems and procedures for domestic and international staff and customers.

2. Clarify sales reporting for products / titles integrated into Newco titles -- combined sales reporting.

3. Resolve conflicting distributor relationships with ABC Group.

4. Develop effective communication strategy for all constituencies (e.g. employees, authors, vendors, etc.)

5. Identify behaviors that drive targeted business performa effectiveness and establish incentives to reinforce th

6. Develop and implement the post-acquisition organizatic including sales regions and management teams.

7. Develop retention/stay bonus plans that are consistent

8. Consolidate Publishing X publishing and corporate serv Newco or Publishing Y facilities by Jan. 1, 1997.

9. Establish data integrity, especially for sales and invento

10. Roll-out and integr

11. Prioritize current IS

12. Design a new bene

13. Complete base sa competitiveness company.

14. Complete the integ

15. Organize company priorities.

16. Reconfigure sales

17. Provide historical it (sales reps, sal

18. Complete prelimin

19. Relocate product li

20. Identify intergroup

21. Identify and secure

22. Develop 1997 (and

Value Driver Analysis

Although value drivers are unique to each transition, the three steps for identifying them are fairly standard.

Step 1: Get All the Key Executives and Managers to Ante Up with Information

The best way to get this information is to sit down with each of the best content experts you have in each line and staff function and ask for it. A value driver interview usually takes a couple of hours, followed up by a few faxes and phone calls. The data gathered address the following three questions:

1. What actions, within your own area(s) of responsibility and control, should be taken to increase revenue, decrease cost, or otherwise capture the value in the deal (or major change)? The actions identified might relate to revenue, operating expense, cost of goods sold, fixed capital investment, working capital investment, cost of capital, or effective tax rate.

2. For each action identified, what is your guesstimate of the quantitative impact (on revenue operating expense, cost of goods sold, and so on), the time frame, and the assumptions underlying your guesstimate of impact (for example, units sold through the new channel, volume savings on purchases, capital expenditures or onetime costs required)? Use these assumptions to calculate a simple measure of shareholder value for each action (such as free cash flow).

3. To assess the probability of success of each action identify (a) its interdependencies with other actions (e.g., cross-selling may require additional, time-consuming training and preparation of collateral materials), (b) obstacles that would have to be over-

come (regulatory approvals for new product offerings), and (c) resources required for implementation (recruiting of technical staff, cash for capital purchases). Use these assumptions to arrive at an estimate of probability of success for the action in question.

Step 2: Rank the Value Drivers

Use the data captured in the value driver interviews to convert estimates and assumptions into a simple measure of shareholder value (for example, free cash flow), and rank each value-driving action based on its financial impact and probability of success.

Step 3: Make the Decision to Concentrate Resources

Conduct a value driver working session. The purpose is to build among the senior executive team commitment and consensus on the key post-deal actions and the relative impact they are likely to have on value creation. This is a critical outcome. In most mergers it's the first time each member of the new executive team has had a common information base from which to carry on a meaningful dialogue about priorities. Without this data, decisions tend to be driven by dominant anecdote. The accessibility of financial and probability-of-success data reduces embarrassing gaps in information, minimizes emotional tirades, and clarifies interdependencies. This supports open dialogue and informed group decision making.

Most important, the value driver working session engenders agreement on what path to take. It accomplishes this by enabling the executive team to candidly explore alternative views of the value drivers, constructively evaluate and rate the value drivers, test assumptions, validate ideas, and build consensus on the 20 percent of actions that will drive 80 percent of the value with the greatest probability of success.

SWAGs (Scientific Wild-Assed Guesses) with senior managers' finger-prints all over them, than iron-clad facts untouched by human hands.

Ownership of the data is more important than decimal-point accuracy. This is not supposed to be an exercise in precision. It's an exercise in establishing the relative value of alternative actions.

When the team reviews the final value driver grid, there are usually some surprising results.

For example, the president of one telecommunications enterprise was surprised to find that one of her favorite marketing ideas, an electronic kiosk, didn't make the cut. It was neither high-financial-impact nor high-probability-of-success. None of the senior executives had wanted to tell her this before the session, even though they all were lukewarm to the idea. Though somewhat deflated, she abided by the process and agreed to shelve the project in the interest of rapidly executing actions for which there was consensus on value creation.

Another example involved a marketing executive who had been campaigning for months to introduce a new product. His very persistence had invited resistance. The new product was a modest revision to an existing product. It wasn't very glamorous, but this executive felt that the company could capture an attractive share of the market in a relatively short time frame with a modest investment of resources. This product development initiative was medium to high on the financial impact scale and high on the probability-of-success scale. The executive team discovered that the product was clearly in the company's value driver strike zone. It took only a few minutes of discussion to agree to the funding of a new product initiative that months of direct persuasion had failed to secure.

Invariably, this process reveals quite a few actions that are consuming resources and have no business doing so. Usually these actions are believed to be opportunistic quick wins, but in reality they simply dilute effort. The probability of success is high, but the economic and transition value is low.

Why do people waste time on these low priorities when there are clearly better uses for the same time and money? The rationale sounds like the old vaudeville routine in which one fellow is down on his hands and knees under a streetlamp, looking for something. Another fellow walks up and asks, "What did you lose?" "My house key," the first one replies.

The passerby kneels down to help search, but neither of them finds anything. Finally the passerby asks, "Are you sure you dropped them here?"

"No, I dropped them across the street," the first fellow says.

"So why are you looking here?" the passerby asks.

The first fellow answers: "The light's better."

More than a few companies behave in this fashion. They lose their perspective when a high-pressure transition confronts them. Management caught spinning its wheels is almost invariably management that is pursuing too many business initiatives simultaneously (some of which are invariably hopeless or valueless), while it allows itself to be distracted by the day-to-day details of infrastructure housekeeping.

They justify this behavior with the following rationale. "Well, given the uncertainties, we need to move on several fronts. We're not willing to bet the farm on just a few." They fail to recognize that they've already made a high-stakes, low-odds bet by launching the transition in the first place. Unless they concentrate their resources on the value-driving actions, they will piddle those resources away on myriad distractions. Like our vaudevillian, they'll spend time and money where the light's better while the keys to their future lie across the street.

> "We moved rapidly even at the risk of making some mistakes. And we don't seem to have made any more mistakes than if we had taken twice as long."
>
> —*Jeremy Strachan, Director of Legal and Corporate Affairs, Glaxo (on the merger with Wellcome)*, Financial Times, *May 22, 1996*

Concentrating resources on the value drivers is not a onetime event. The process described here often becomes part of management's ongoing practice. The expression "value drivers" frequently becomes part of the company's lexicon, and the stories of shelved "hobby horses" and discovered ideas take their place as part of the company's folklore.

Value driver analysis is the heart of an accelerated transition. It also is the foundation for all subsequent actions to stabilize the company, build momentum, and capture early wins. It provides the charters for the transition teams, determines the criteria for structuring the organization, defines the events around which a behavior-based culture can be built, provides guidance in deploying people, and sets the standard for determining incentives.

Most important, value driver analysis is not only the foundation for an accelerated transition but the foundation for how a company makes decisions and takes action long into the future. This realization prompted one enthusiastic CEO to say: "If it doesn't advance a value driver, I'm going to shoot it, sell it, or ignore it."

We couldn't agree more.

6

Windshield Watching in Seattle

Early Communication and Stability

The CEO stared at the press release. It was pretty good work, and it took only three rounds of revisions.

Global Computer and Nexus Systems announced today that an agreement to merge has been reached by the two boards of directors. The transaction, valued at over $1.2 billion, will be financed with a combination of debt and stock.

"This is going to put us in a very strong position to grow internationally and ensure that the next generation of high-end servers and workstations leads the market and sets the standard," said John Woodstock, chairman and CEO of Global Computers, Inc., a Palo Alto–based company. "It will drive the high returns that our shareholders have come to expect," he added.

"This is a perfect fit," said John T. Wu, founder and president of Seattle-based Nexus Systems. "Global offers the reputation, distribution channels, and management experience we need to grow the current product line and position our new products for global leadership. We are confident that Global's hardware and our networking software will offer

customers an unparalleled advantage in speed, interconnectivity, and overall functionality."

The shareholders of both companies are expected to approve the merger at a specially scheduled meeting next month.

*John Woodstock looked at his watch. He'd been thinking about this
press release for forty-five minutes.*

*I wonder what my daughter will say when she sees this, he thought
to himself. Probably, "Congratulations, Dad, I guess this means our
summer hiking trip is off. It's okay, I understand, we'll do it again next
year."*

*And what about my neighbor Fred? "Nice going, buddy. Now don't
work too hard. Remember what happened to me last spring when that
Dutch firm bought my company. Chest pains and an ulcer."*

*John shifted in his chair, imagining what some of Global's "plat-
inum" account customers might be thinking. "Should I buy now or wait
for the new release? Will prices go up? Will Global meet its delivery
commitments? Will service response times get longer? Should we start
qualifying other suppliers?"*

*And what about Global's key suppliers? What will they be thinking?
he wondered. "Will Global be changing vendors? Will they change our
specifications, again, to accommodate the Nexus configuration requirements? Will they pay on time? Will they be able to pay on time?"*

*What about our employees in Silicon Valley and in Seattle? I can just
hear them now, John thought. "Everybody knows we don't need two of
everything. Who'll stay? Who'll go? Who'll be in charge of what? Who'll
get promoted?" Even the ones who know they have secure jobs will
have questions. "Will my development project continue to be funded?
What will happen to the new equipment purchase order? Should I cancel my vacation? Will the new dental plan cover orthodontia?"*

*And what about our distributors? The local press? The trade associ-
ations? Even the Philippine and Irish governments—will be wondering
what impact this will have on Global's announced plans to expand our
facilities in their countries.*

*There would be lots of questions from lots of people. John looked
back down at the piece of paper on his desk. This press release doesn't*

answer any of them! Not even remotely! And while everybody is spending time wondering and worrying, they won't be investing, buying, supplying, designing, manufacturing, selling, or supporting us. And if all these stakeholders don't do what we need them to do, this deal will be worth less than the paper it's printed on.

So why are we sending out this press release? He could hear his PR director's response: "John, we need to announce to the press, to the public, to the world, what this deal is about. We've got an exciting story to tell, a whole new value proposition for our customers, employees, and investors. We've got to tell that story! We need to send a convincing message to the world about the new Global-Nexus. We need to seize the opportunity while people are listening and take advantage of the publicity!"

"A convincing message to the world," John thought. Well, that it was. But just who would we be convincing? He had a nagging suspicion that the only people who would be convinced would be the people who wrote the press release. They didn't need convincing.

What about the other stakeholders? What about the concerned customers, nervous suppliers, anxious employees, suspicious regulators, skeptical press, and cautious investors? If they didn't accept and support this deal, he and his new Global-Nexus leadership team would be in for some heavy sledding.

John stood up and began walking around his office. How are we going to convince all these different and important groups of people? How can we get their attention and win their support? He stopped pacing for a moment and looked down at the press release. He thought to himself, I'm not sure very many of the people who really matter are going to read this thing. In fact, if they do read it, I'm sure they will see it for what it is. Hype!

John looked at his watch again. He'd been stewing over this press release for over an hour! He picked up the phone. This wasn't going to work. Something had to be done.

Most executives don't think or act the way John did. Either they spend too much time on the press release, hyping the deal, or they delegate virtually all of the communication and PR effort to a sub-

ordinate and then start tackling the next crisis on their overcommit-
ted schedule.

When customers, suppliers, investors, and employees start raising
questions, most executives are not prepared. The questions come in real
time. The answers are usually improvised, and the results are predictable—
more confusion, more uncertainty, more anxiety, and more cost.

Hyping, equivocating, and hip-shooting tend to be the dominant tac-

---

The Cost of Confusion

You are the acquirer. You have two thousand employees in your
company. Assume that each one of them is well informed, very secure, and spends only thirty minutes a day wondering, speculating,
and trading gossip with other employees about how the deal will
affect them. That comes to one thousand hours of lost productivity per day, five thousand hours a week, and twenty thousand
hours a month.

Add to that calculation the one thousand employees in the acquired company, who are probably feeling less secure and are
spending, conservatively, one hour per day wondering, speculating,
and trading gossip about the future. That comes to an additional
twenty thousand hours per month in lost productivity—a combined total of forty thousand hours.

At an average compensation rate of $40 per hour, it's costing
you $1.6 million per month (perhaps $2.4 million fully loaded) in
lost productivity, not counting the impact of deteriorating customer relations and delayed sales due to unanswered phone calls,
missed schedules, and turnover of talented people.

As the acquirer, you're paying a substantial hidden premium.
The cost can be minimized by reducing gossip, rumor, and speculation as rapidly as possible. This requires proactive communication to all stakeholders on the post-deal issues that are most
relevant to them.

tics for managing communication during a major transition. The messages are usually 99 percent content-free. They are more about making pronouncements than connecting with people. They emphasize style over substance and confuse talking with communicating. Most important, they fail to connect with the real information needs of employees, customers, suppliers, investors, and other stakeholders.

Effective communication during a transition is about securing stakeholder understanding and acceptance. It's about building support for a new business proposition among *all* the stakeholders who are expected to buy into and deliver the new proposition. It's about minimizing the crippling effects of uncertainty on performance. It's about keeping people focused and energized rather than confused and perplexed. When investors, customers, suppliers, and employees spend time worrying and wondering, they aren't spending time investing, buying, supplying, or producing.

Critics and Molehill Men

Unfortunately, nearly all mergers, acquisitions, and large-scale changes are announced before implementation plans are developed. Consequently, when the first torrent of questions hits frazzled corporate executives, they simply clam up. They assume it's better to say nothing than to say something from which they may have to extract themselves later. Sensible as this might seem, it makes matters worse.

Within days, sometimes hours, of the announcement suspicion grows that management is withholding negative information from employees. Why? The reasoning is obvious to the newly paranoid: "If there were good news, they'd be telling us." The sounds of silence don't last very long. The void gets filled with wild speculation—rumor and gossip fabricated from the prophecies of internal critics.

Post-deal speculation feeds on paranoia, evolves into misinterpretation, and grows in complexity until it becomes a multiheaded monster. Rumors and partial truths quickly mutate out of control and drive down the prospects of the most promising ventures. Yesterday's suspicion turns into today's gossip, tomorrow's scandal, and next week's crisis.

> **"If we had been as creative in developing new products as we were in creating new rumors, we probably would have been the acquirer rather than the acquired."**
>
> *V.P. of manufacturing
> for an East Coast consumer
> products company*

And who is fanning the flames of speculation? The critics. Nearly every management team has a few disgruntled critics. The uncertainty surrounding the transition brings them out in force. Armed with an attitude and almost no information, these critics feast on management's silence. They provide their own explanations for why information is being withheld and why decisions aren't being announced. Anxious and frustrated employees are all too eager to listen. If you're a critic, this is the audience you've always dreamed of having.

Many of these critics resemble what the late humorist Fred Allen used to call the molehill men. A molehill man is someone who arrives at his office at 8:00 A.M. and finds a molehill on his desk. He has until 5:00 P.M. to turn it into a mountain. A really effective molehill man can finish his work by noon and spend the rest of the day terrorizing the organization with his own personal distortions of reality—thus driving up anxiety, driving down productivity, and fostering an environment that proves his point.

When management announces a change and follows it with silence or, worse yet, equivocal statements and pleas for time to sort things out, they allow dozens, sometimes hundreds, of molehills to proliferate. In essence, they provide the critics with a platform and an open microphone. The molehill men quickly establish themselves as the best source of data and the arbiters of justice for information-deprived stakeholders.

Just like a bad soap opera, the plot thickens as twisted logic ignites a search for data to verify the most negative rumors. People become absolutely compulsive about filling in information gaps and can think of little else. Employees drop other tasks to talk with co-workers and superiors, comb the trade press, review Wall Street

> **A molehill man is someone who arrives at his office at 8:00 A.M. and finds a molehill on his desk. He has until 5:00 P.M. to turn it into a mountain.**

Windshield Watching in Seattle

It was a time of uncertainty over the cold war and concerns about Soviet nuclear testing, of rising awareness about ecology and the delicate balance between big business and the fragile environment.

Suddenly the Seattle area was seized by epidemic hysteria—what psychologists call a mass psychosis. Military intelligence experts smelled a sinister plot to destabilize the government, and out-of-office politicians sniffed sweet opportunity as the rumors multiplied.

What strange phenomenon stirred such distress among the normally unflappable souls of the Evergreen State? Automobile windshields—or, more precisely, the tiny pockmarks mysteriously cropping up on windshield after windshield, as if caused by a plague. As word of the scarring spread, more and more people checked their windshields and—horror of horrors—discovered the same damage.

With each passing day the anxiety increased, and the absence of answers seemed ominous and frightening to the citizenry. Two dominant theories emerged from among the rumors and rampant speculation: the nuclear fallout theory and the macadam theory.

Recent atomic testing by the Soviet Union fueled the fallout theory. Adherents maintained that the Soviets had contaminated the atmosphere, and with Seattle's moist climate as a catalyst, the nuclear fallout had spread a glass-etching acid across the Pacific Northwest. Who knew what other sinister side effects could yet appear?

The macadam theory—undoubtedly the favorite of certain local politicians—sprouted from the governor's aggressive highway development initiative, which had produced hundreds of miles of macadamized roads treated with environmentally objectionable chemicals. Petrochemical binders in the roadbeds, so the theory went, combined with Seattle's nearly constant dampness to create a layer of acidic moisture on the highway surface, there to be thrown up on unsuspecting windshields by the spinning tires of passing cars.

Faced with a political nightmare, the governor sought the help of President Eisenhower. Washington coughed up a team of experts from the National Bureau of Standards to sort out the problem and stanch the growing hysteria. The search for solutions was on.

To everyone's surprise, the NBS's scientific minds applied their statistical tools and measurement acumen to neither theory. Instead, they trained their sights on a much more mundane—and certainly less emotional—explanation involving the historical incidence of windshield pitting. After careful analysis of geographic differences, time-interval comparisons, and other objective factors, the conclusion was unassailable: there was no abnormal windshield pitting in Seattle at all, just normal wear and tear on exposed surfaces.

Seattle had been seized not by a plague of windshield pitting but by an epidemic of windshield watching. It seems that as reports of pitting had spread, more and more car owners checked their windshields for evidence of the damage. Looking at the glass from the outside rather than from the inside, as they normally would while driving, they noticed the minor damage that was always there but usually went unnoticed.

Someone's casual observation of windshield pitting generated first speculation, then rumor, and eventually mass hysteria.

Panic is not limited to Washingtonians and windshields. Corporate transitions are case studies in employee uncertainty and anxiety. Few things drive distress, edginess, and misperception more than a merger, acquisition, or large-scale change.

The first announcement comes as either a surprise or an anticlimax because it had been long expected. Generally it is virtually content-free—mostly promotion and hype. It is seldom more detailed than a press release covering the basics of the deal and a few cursory references to business opportunity, cost savings, and competitive advantage. Usually there is a promise of details to come. But details seldom come soon enough.

> Minor events are imbued with great meaning. Simple mistakes become sinister plots. Unrelated events become causal links.
>
> Absent real information, people fill in the blanks with their own information. Fueled by fear, uncertainty, and doubt, the answers they create are invariably far worse than the reality that awaits them.

analyst reports, or, if necessary, question key customers or suppliers who may have access to better information. Concerned customers, in turn, query employees, other customers, or go directly to board members. With everyone so anxious and distracted, business suffers.

Wild Speculation

In an environment devoid of meaningful information, trivial events assume monumental importance. Wracked with uncertainty, employees interpret everything from the bleakest perspective. A department meeting with fifteen invited participants and twelve chairs fuels speculation of lost jobs. The sudden appearance of "suits" in a casual R&D environment generates rumors of funding cuts or of new demands to justify continuing research.

The spiral of supposition can take on almost farcical tones. Consider, for example, the case of a $200 million California-based manufacturer that, in the midst of its best year, surprised everyone with the announcement that it would be acquired by an East Coast conglomerate and merged into one of the acquirer's divisions. The announcement was a simple press release read at an employee meeting with a promise of details to come.

Within a day of the announcement a rumor surfaced that the company's well-respected president had been fired. As he walked through the plant, employees approached him offering sincere regrets over his misfortune, inquiring about his plans for the future, and wondering whether their own jobs were secure. Totally baffled by these sympathies, he assured everyone who approached him that he intended to stay. He reminded them that he was the surviving CEO and asked where they had gotten their misinformation. No one seemed to know how the rumor had begun.

Despite the CEO's protests to the contrary, by the end of the day there were murmurs of layoffs and whispers of union organizing activity. By the next morning there was speculation that the plant would be closed, all production would be outsourced in Latin America, and the callous acquirer would even deny employees the formal notifications required by the federal government under the Warren Act. By that afternoon the inventory manager heard that a group of employees had decided to retain a labor attorney to prepare a formal complaint to the U.S. Labor Department. By day's end the vice president of manufacturing noticed a precipitous drop in production output.

The next morning, amid urgent calls from angry and confused customers, stern state officials, frantic municipal authorities, and a singularly irritating representative of the electrical workers' union, several executives met with the CEO to sort out the growing crisis. A brief comparison of rumors quickly identified the event that sparked the firestorm of speculative hysteria.

Here is what really happened. On the morning after the announcement the president took his Mercedes in for servicing. The auto dealership provided him with a Ford Taurus to drive in the meantime. When he arrived at the plant in the Taurus, he found a delivery truck blocking his reserved parking space. So he drove to the rear of the building and parked in a space near the back door.

Arriving at his office, he found the furniture piled outside the door

---

Effective transition communication is based on three simple principles:

1. Silence is not an option, even if you don't have all the answers.
2. You must know and verify what stakeholders are most concerned about.
3. You must have an integrated information strategy that addresses stakeholders' concerns, builds on their hopes, and speaks to them through channels they trust, in terms they can understand.

and remembered that the maintenance staff had cleaned the carpets in his office the night before and they would still be damp. Needing to make several calls to European buyers, he commandeered the vacant office of a production scheduler. By the time he emerged from the office, a rumor had spread throughout the plant that he had been stripped of the privileges of his office and would soon be gone for good. Events that only two weeks earlier would have been overlooked now conspired to create a crisis with wide-ranging implications.

Confusion has a miraculous capacity to stimulate the search for clues and clarity. These employees had been surprised by the announcement of the deal and left in the dark about what would happen next. Confused and anxious, they became hyper-alert and began to search for signs, clues, any indication, even a tenuous one, as to what might happen next.

In an environment devoid of information, all clues, regardless of how shallow or misleading, are treated as valuable parts to the puzzle. In an information-rich environment the search for clues is suppressed, distraction is minimized, and stability can be maintained. When it comes to fueling speculation and rumor, few motivators are as powerful as the anxiety and uncertainty fostered by a lack of information.

The Big Hype

One surefire way of building distrust among stakeholders is to take a public relations approach to transition communications. While crafting the right "spin" for a message, public relations and marketing communications staff typically bury the meaningful content in a morass of hype. As a result, they fail to connect with the employees and customers, who usually have their crap detectors on high gain after the first content-free announcement. When the spin has been filtered out, there is seldom much satisfying content left.

Consider the following true story.

Andrew was truly proud and pleased with himself. He believed he had created the ultimate merger communication strategy. His ticket to the Cleos. A guaranteed Golden Quill Award.

Covering the walls of the conference room were beautiful proof copies of posters—Batman and Robin, Fred Astaire and Ginger Rogers, Spencer Tracy and Katharine Hepburn, Clark Gable and Vivien Leigh. Each poster carried the headline: "Great marriages in history." The final poster showed a tandem bicycle with the two CEOs, happily pedaling, above the caption "Another great combination."

"Pretty good, huh?" Andrew asked, expecting kudos.

"Well, Andrew, this is pretty clever stuff, but do the employees really need to be convinced that the two companies make a good team? Or are they more concerned about other things?" asks an advisor.

"That's not the point of this campaign. We are trying to convince employees and investors that this is a good deal."

"That's an important objective, but this may not be the best way to achieve it. By not answering the real questions, people may begin to question your motives."

"Why would they become suspicious of our motives?"

"Because the campaign is working too hard to compare this deal with other great combinations, rather than provide a sound rationale for how this merger benefits all the stakeholders—customers, employees, vendors, suppliers, investors, whole communities where your plants are major employers. Everybody knows that the plants are not operating to capacity, that the product lines overlap, that you have redundant staff, different sales strategies, and totally different computer systems, not to mention dramatically different cultures. To even the casual observer this spells cuts, chaos, and confusion."

"Do you know how much time went into creating these posters?"

"Andrew they are clever and creative posters. Clearly, a lot of energy was invested, but something more than a PR campaign is needed. People are preoccupied with trying to figure out what this means to them. This is what needs to be addressed, starting now!"

"What do you mean? I don't understand."

"Communication is much more than telling people what you want them to think and know. It's got a much sharper edge. Good communication is about preserving market share, company strengths, brand reputation, goodwill, and all the other intangible assets in a deal. It's

protection of the home base. It's survival. Shareholder value is lost more precipitously in transition periods than at any other time in a company's life, and the battle can be won or lost on whether you capture the support of the employees. Poor communication is one of the top killers of post-deal value creation."

"So what else should we do?"

"Start with gaining an understanding of what all the stakeholders know and don't know about the deal. Get the answers to a number of questions. What have you heard about the merger? What is your understanding of why the deal is being done? What advantages do you see in the merger? What are your major concerns? What is your perception of the other company? How do you think the other company perceives your company?"

"To whom are we directing these questions?"

"The stakeholders. Employees, investors, suppliers, customers, community leaders in locations where facilities are located, and any other groups directly affected by this deal. This will not only get valuable information about current perceptions, it will also make it clear that the company's leadership is concerned, listening, and responsible. People will feel included and respected. Also, this way early urgent concerns can be identified and responses developed before simple questions and misunderstandings become public relations disasters."

"But we already know what they probably are thinking about. Why should we waste time and money trying to find out something we already know the answer to?"

"Even if it's clear today what their concerns are, by tomorrow those concerns will have mutated, fueled by speculation, fear, incomplete information, rumors, and outspoken critics. Even now, fertile and panicky minds are creating bizarre interpretations and phobic misconstructions that would boggle your mind. A reporter asks an Albuquerque production employee if she is worried about losing her job. Two hours later rumors of layoffs are spreading through the Austin, Sunnyvale, and Albuquerque plants. A key customer reads about the merger in the Wall Street Journal. *Anxious about deliveries, he calls to check the status of a big shipment. The phone is constantly busy because of an unrelated com-*

munications problem. Concerned about the interruption of supply, he schedules an appointment with a competitor's sales representative."

"If it's changing so fast, why bother asking anybody anything?"

"By quickly identifying the core concerns, you can address critical issues before they morph into monsters. This enables you to build a comprehensive communication plan that spells out what needs to be communicated, to which audiences, and through which channels. This will help calm frayed nerves, garner support, maintain open dialogue, and put the company's leaders in control of the information network."

"Okay, but what am I going to do with these posters?"

"Sign them, frame them, and put them in the CEO's office. There might come a time when he'll need a reminder of how good a deal this was."

Hip-Shooting—The Content-Free Executive

Many executives don't need a PR hack to help them make fools of themselves. They are perfectly capable of doing it on their own.

Usually by the time senior management realizes that communication has been given insufficient priority, they are being criticized by stakeholders as either inept communicators—insensitive and slow to reveal essential information—or deceptive manipulators who have deliberately withheld information. This communication failure and the perceptions it promotes makes a challenging transition more difficult. It fosters frustration, mistrust, alienation, and withdrawal among stakeholders—hardly a positive outcome.

At this point nearly all management communication becomes reactive. Executives find themselves spending more and more time responding to or avoiding stakeholder demands for information and less and less time in control of the exchange. In an effort to regain control, they step up the number of site visits to each other's locations. These visits increase their visibility and accessibility and should improve employee perceptions, if they prepare properly. But they seldom do.

For whatever reason—self-confidence, hubris, ineptitude—many executives commit the recurring cardinal sin of showing up unprepared or, at best, insufficiently prepared for site visits to acquired firms. They are seldom fully informed on the issues and concerns of the key people, not to mention the workforce. And if by chance they have been briefed on the issues, they rarely have sufficient background information to discuss them meaningfully. Instead, they think they can get by on charm and wit.

Many executives are indeed charming, witty, and glib. In the post-deal environment charm is an asset, and wit can smooth the

Four firm rules—no secrets, no surprises, no hype, no empty promises.

way. But nothing—not even charm and wit—can save a content-free executive from fanning the flames of resentment. Leaders who are unprepared to answer basic, easily anticipated questions are disparaged or, even worse, disregarded. They foster alienation. Sensing they have erred, they usually make matters worse by attempting to reduce tension (usually their own) with ad-lib humor or flip answers.

One CEO at a Silicon Valley technology company decided to visit the engineering group of a company his business had recently acquired. Word was out that the best people were being recruited by competitors. Being a man of action, supremely impatient, and confident in his charm and enthusiasm, he packed his bag and flew off to win the hearts and minds of his acquired engineers.

Unprepared to address the substance of their concerns—loss of engineering managers, insufficient and poorly trained staff, aging workstations, conflicting development philosophies, friction over marketing strategy, dissatisfaction with compensation, and dissension over business direction—his only plan was to be effusive about their accomplishments and promise to redesign their incentive compensation.

In the first half-hour he told them about his vision. In the next ten minutes he effused about their accomplishments. In the following three minutes he informed them that a new incentive plan would be designed. Forty-three minutes into his visit and with nothing further to say, he solicited their questions and concerns.

He spent the next hour nodding sagely, responding cryptically, attempting humor, and generally shooting from the hip. In short, he had no answers—not even short ones. When he sensed that the engineers were not impressed, he tried to sweep them up with his enthusiasm. (It had always worked back home.) As the meeting ended, he reemphasized how happy he was that they were now one family and promised to commit whatever resources were necessary to combine the two companies' technologies into a "superior product." He shook hands with everyone as they left the room.

One week later two more engineers left the company and another had given notice of his departure. At an exit interview they claimed that all they could remember from the meeting with the CEO was his unwillingness to share answers he undoubtedly had and his implication at the end of the session that they did not already have a superior product.

Did they learn their lesson? Not a chance. Executives began to descend on the acquired company like a traveling circus. Few bothered to prepare. Most relied on their charm. It was never enough.

One marketing executive was asked the following question in a large group of assembled employees. "We've heard that you have no respect for employees' private lives and that rewards go to people who dedicate nearly every waking moment to the company." In a vain attempt at humor, the visiting executive said, "That's not true. We're very flexible in our expectations. You can work any eighteen hours of the day that you choose." There was no laughter.

In three months engineering was decimated, customer service was crippled, and marketing was nearly nonexistent. Their competitors were sending them thank-you notes and customers were sending "Dear John" letters.

Transition communication is about more than backslapping and ego-boosting. It's about mobilizing support and removing uncertainty. It's about honesty and candor. It's about supplying honest answers to the hard questions that good people ask when they're in the dark and worried, as in a major acquisition or restructuring. Straight talk itself is a highly important value driver. It's anchored to four firm rules—no secrets, no surprises, no hype, no empty promises.

7

No Secrets,
No Surprises, No Hype,
No Empty Promises

Connecting with Your Stakeholders

When organizational upheaval begins, with all its attendant fear, loathing, and paranoia, nothing is less helpful than one-way pronouncements that raise more questions than they answer. Two-way talk is absolutely essential. It's never too early to launch dialogues on all fronts for the simple reason that support wanes fast; opposition multiplies even faster. Unhappiness is contagious.

Communications that Stabilize and Mobilize the Company

Securing stakeholder acceptance and support for the change is one of the most powerful ways to stabilize the company during the transition period. It helps to accelerate the transition and drive higher levels of performance.

The recent PricewaterhouseCoopers survey of 124 mergers and acquisitions provides dramatic support for this conclusion. Companies that implemented an effective post-deal communications strategy shortly after announcing the change reported significantly better results in such areas as customer focus, employee commitment, clarity of company direction, speed of decision making, and productivity than did those that delayed implementation of a communication strategy for three months or more.

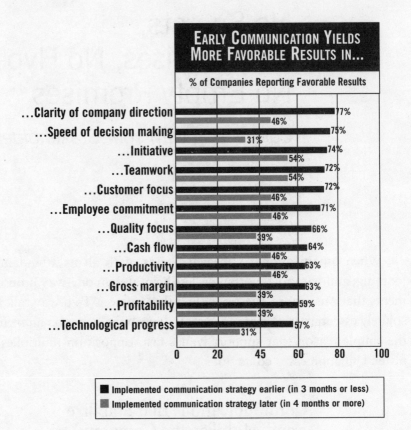

Secure Support and Capture Buy-in

The communication of change is not about announcements. It's about gaining support and capturing buy-in. Candid communication is a defensive perimeter and tactical edge—not just to transmit information or even to create awareness, but to build stakeholder acceptance, early support, and full participation. It must be wielded like a weapon, a powerful tool for establishing leadership and direction and rallying the troops to the cause.

Successful communication of change begins by understanding that the questions following any announcement revolve around one central theme: "How does this affect me?" All stakeholders, the people who influence and are influenced by the actions of your company—employees, customers, managers, investors, suppliers, and even the community at large—quickly begin to speculate about the implications for them.

> **Candid communication is your defensive perimeter and tactical edge—not just to transmit information or even to create awareness, but to build stakeholder acceptance, early support, and full participation. It must be wielded like a weapon, a powerful tool for establishing leadership and direction and rallying the troops to the cause.**

Employees ordinarily speculate about job security, income opportunity, personal influence, and career opportunity. Customers typically speculate about changes in price, quality, responsiveness, timely delivery, credit policies, and alternative sources of supply. Suppliers generally speculate about having to resubmit competitive bids, changes in policy on payables aging, new purchasing agreements, and changes in ordering practices, volume, and delivery demands.

Shareholders and stock analysts speculate on the validity of management's reasons for doing the deal, whether announcement hype is covering up an unjustifi-

> **Competitors are taking advantage of the confusion and conjuring a downside message for anyone who will listen.**

able purchase price, and when, or if, they will see a return on the investment. State and municipal authorities speculate on the economic impact of the deal on the local economy, tax coffers, and the drain on public funds for social entitlements like unemployment insurance, welfare, and workers' compensation.

The press is speculating on angles for local stories and trying to find out who to contact both within and outside of the companies. And while all of this is going on, competitors are taking advantage of the confusion and conjuring a downside message for anyone who will listen.

All of this speculation is immediate and concurrent with the announcement itself. Consequently, only a fraction of the message is absorbed, and even less is understood in any objective sense. It is colored by personal biases, concerns, and misconstructions. The speculated scenario becomes the reality—the distorted reality—that influences stakeholder perception, drives behavior, molds workforce attitudes, shapes post-deal performance, and influences the outcome of the transition.

Listen to the Stakeholders

You can either control the speculation or become a victim of it. Stakeholder analysis is both your first line of defense and your first step in taking control. It demonstrates that company executives are serious about understanding stakeholder issues and addressing key concerns. It provides people who are probably feeling helpless, ignored, and justifiably resentful with an opportunity to speak out and participate in the changes taking place. It guides the development of effective and cost-efficient communications tactics. It also helps protect the customer base from assaults by competitors that may be more informed about customer concerns.

Because no two mergers are alike and because the effects of large-scale change vary from company to company and situation to situation, every group of stakeholders has its own mix of concerns. Even savvy acquirers can't anticipate the variety and volume of questions—let alone the range and complexity of the answers that must be formulated. Understanding those concerns is a primary objective of stakeholder analysis. This is not the time to guess.

Stakeholder analysis helps surface the *early urgent concerns* (EUCs) that are creating distractions and disrupting operations, today and maybe tomorrow. They are the things that worry employees and customers. The things that will erupt into crises if not dealt with immediately. EUCs might include misinformation about why the deal was done, the timing of the deal, or false rumors about facilities being closed, products phased out, or projects canceled. Generally these issues can be addressed immediately, with minimal cost and with a clearly positive impact on stakeholder perceptions.

Sort Out the Issues and Kill the Snakes Fast

Stakeholder analysis involves three steps. First, identify all the stakeholder groups across all the locations. Stakeholders are individuals and groups who influence and are influenced by the actions of the company. They include your customers, suppliers, contractors, strategic partners, and major investors.

Second, gather data quickly from as many stakeholder segments as time and resources permit. The best way to unearth EUCs is to use focus groups, interviews, or surveys. This should be done as soon after the announcement as possible. It should be repeated (at least with the employee group) in two months if the transition is dragging or enthusiasm has waned or failed to grow.

The focus groups and interviews are for collecting feedback and should not be used as a venue for clarifying past messages. Ask your stakeholders: What is your understanding of the reason for the deal? How have you interpreted the recent announcements? Do you see value for yourself in the deal? If so, where? If not, why not? Have you been told how the change affects you and other stakeholders? What are your perceptions of the other company? What have you heard from other customers, suppliers, business partners? What are your concerns? What would spark your enthusiasm? What challenges do you see ahead?

Ask your stakeholders: What is your understanding of the reason for the deal? . . . Do you see value for yourself in the deal? . . . Have you been told how the change affects you and other stakeholders? What are your perceptions of the other company? What have you heard from other customers, suppliers, business partners? What are your concerns? What would spark your enthusiasm? What challenges do you see ahead?

When the answers to these questions are sorted by stakeholder group, you get a reasonably accurate impression of whether your communications have been received and how they have been perceived. You quickly learn whether messages have been misinterpreted, misconstrued, or misdirected, or whether they just missed the mark. You learn the concerns of each stakeholder group and what it will take to win each group's support and cooperation during the transition. Therefore, the third step in stakeholder analysis is to consolidate the information and build a database of clear statements of concerns, perceptions, and preferred communication channels by stakeholder group.

If the planned communications are not likely to build support, acceptance, and understanding among important stakeholder groups, then they must be revised or eliminated. This is one of the most effective ways to prevent public relations and communication advocates from over-engineering their solutions and simply introducing more noise into an already clamorous situation.

This analysis of stakeholder response is the central plank in a communications platform going forward. But most important, it enables you to identify the EUCs that must be quickly addressed.

If a snake crawled into your home, you wouldn't convene a committee to determine its genus and species and how best to dispose of it. You would grab a stick and kill it, right? The same solution applies to EUCs. Identify them fast and eliminate them fast—or lose support fast.

Senior executives often resist the idea of focus groups. Their resistance can usually be traced to one or more of the following reasons:

1. Blind arrogance—the executive who thinks she knows everything the stakeholders are going to say.
2. Fear—the executive who is scared to death of what he might hear.
3. Apathy—the executive who just doesn't care and doesn't want to find out anything new because then she'll have to respond (which will just add pressure to her life).
4. Ignorance—the executive who just doesn't get it and probably never will.
5. Myopic miserliness—the executive who expends enormous sums of money and invests vast sums in goodwill that he will never recapture, only to spend very little to make the deal work.
6. Distrust—The executive who believes focus groups will only give employees a forum to "bitch, moan, and stir up trouble."

The Refrigerator Fallacy

The communication of change more often aggravates, rather than reduces, anxiety and uncertainty. The management team frequently falls prey to the refrigerator fallacy and the false assumption of communication that it fosters. When you close a refrigerator door, you know, intellectually, that the little light on the inside switches off. But you can never be sure without opening the door. When you do so, the light is on. You have to trust in the manufacturer of the refrigerator.

Trusting the simple mechanical switch in a refrigerator is not the same as trusting the complex receiving device between the ears of an employee who has been blindsided by the announcement of a significant change that may dramatically alter familiar routines or derail a career path. Believing that employees and other stakeholders have understood, correctly interpreted, and committed to memory your communications after a single (or even a few) announcements is to fall prey to the refrigerator fallacy. Just saying or writing something does not guarantee that it has been communicated or that it will be accurately recalled.

From the optimistic enthusiasm of the first announcement to the excitement of the closing and the sobering communication of overhead consolidation and cost-cutting, mergers, acquisitions, and large-scale change are emotion-laden events. As such, they represent the greatest of all communications challenges.

You cannot expect people—employees, customers, vendors, shareholders—who are impacted by an event to fully absorb 100 percent—or for that matter, even 50 percent—of the communications content associated with the change.

They visually scan each written message and aurally surf each spoken statement until they find personally relevant content corresponding to their most urgent questions and concerns. The personally relevant content is then chewed from every possible direction as they work through scenarios and speculate about implications.

Unfortunately, some executives never see the light. They only feel the heat.

Don't wait until you get burned. The focus groups and interviews can uncover all sorts of land mines and hidden traps. Moreover, they are the fastest way to check for the refrigerator fallacy, filter noise out of the dialogue with stakeholders, and build support.

Focusing especially on people with a real stake in the organization's future—people with something to gain who will make it all work if they can be shown what's in it for them—not only advances the cause, it also builds public acceptance. The therapeutic effect of letting stakeholders vent, in itself, justifies the effort. Not only do you get right to the heart of the EUCs, but you take a giant step toward winning the hearts of the stakeholders.

Investing up-front effort to understand the depth and breadth of stakeholder concerns, perceptions, and preferences has multiple benefits. It ultimately ensures that investments in communication tactics build stakeholder acceptance rather than monuments to the prowess of the communicators.

Flood the Channels—Andrew Returns

While addressing the EUCs, it's important to build and begin executing the communications plan. The data from the stakeholder analysis form the foundation of this plan . . . as Andrew discovered.

"I don't believe it. When we started the focus groups, I thought we could predict all the important feedback. I half expected this to be a worthless drill. You should have heard the complaints from the managers. Every one of them was certain he knew what the employees were thinking. Who could have known? We thought we were sending E-mail to all the employees. Not one member of the senior staff realized the Chicago office wasn't on e-mail.

"The customer interviews blew everyone away. We sent every customer a letter explaining the deal and how orders would be processed in the future. But not one customer understood it."

Two hundred employees and not a word. None of the top brass knew. No wonder they're talking to the telecommunication workers' union."

"Were there any other surprises?"

"Actually yes. We did learn some important things. Two key R&D projects were almost shut down because someone misinterpreted a comment the CEO made. All the Macintosh programmers have their paper on the street, looking for jobs, because they heard that the new VP of engineering wants all new applications on a Windows platform. Not true. I don't know where they heard this stuff.

"Everyone is confused about the new management structure. Half the staff is moaning about job titles and compensation differences, and everyone figures the CEO sold out. I wouldn't blame him. There's a lot of cash in this deal. But the customer interviews blew everyone away. We sent every customer a letter explaining the deal and how orders would be processed in the future. But not one customer understood it."

"That's important feedback, Andrew. But it'll be worthless unless it is acted upon. Tell everyone what you learned in the focus groups. Formulate responses to their questions and concerns, and build a targeted communications plan."

"It sounds like a lot of work. We don't have the staff or the time to do all that. And it's one more thing added to a list of tasks that's already too long. We learned what we needed from the focus groups and interviews. We'll make some adjustments. People will notice. I think that's enough."

"If you don't act on what you learned in a timely and visible way, and if it's not reflected in current communications, you will have breached the trust that

"If you don't act on what you learned in a timely and visible way, and if it's not reflected in current communications, you will have breached the trust that you've begun to build, and you'll have to start all over again to earn the confidence of your stakeholders. It's going to cost you in goodwill. Once you lose their trust, it's difficult to win back. People gravitate to clarity. It provides coherence and meaning. It attracts support and stabilizes the organization. It reduces distraction, increases focus, and helps everyone get back on track."

"Flood the communications channels with targeted messages. Repeat those messages again and again, to drive home the meaning and minimize misinterpretation. The objective is clarity, quantity, and customization—mass customization of messages. Every group needs to feel that the communication is directed at them. This is a campaign for their hearts and minds."

you've begun to build, and you'll have to start all over again to earn the confidence of your stakeholders. It's going to cost you in goodwill. Once you lose their trust, it's difficult to win back. People gravitate to clarity. It provides coherence and meaning. It attracts support and stabilizes the organization. It reduces distraction, increases focus, and helps everyone get back on track.

"Andrew, you're right. It's a lot of extra work. But it's also an early opportunity to ignite the flame of enthusiasm, mobilize the troops, and drive early gains. Don't blow it."

"All right. All right. No more lectures. Too much is at stake. We can't afford to mess this up. Productivity's down, everyone's stressed out, and it's taking a lot longer to capture those savings than we thought. What's should we do next?"

"Flood the communications channels with targeted messages. Repeat those messages again and again, to drive home the meaning and minimize misinterpretation. The objective is clarity, quantity, and customization—mass customization of messages. Every group needs to feel that the communication is directed at them. This is a campaign for their hearts and minds.

"Start with a simple communications matrix. Down the left side of the matrix list all the business, organizational, and human resource issues relating to the deal: the rationale for the merger, post-deal business strategy, changes in the management structure, plans for accelerating the transition, anticipated revenue enhancements, targeted cost savings, human resource issues like compensation and benefits changes, severance plans, short- and long-term retention incentives, identification and retention of key people, policy and procedure shifts, interim decisions like credit policy, early plans like consolidation of sales territories, and so on. The initial list will be long and it will get longer over time."

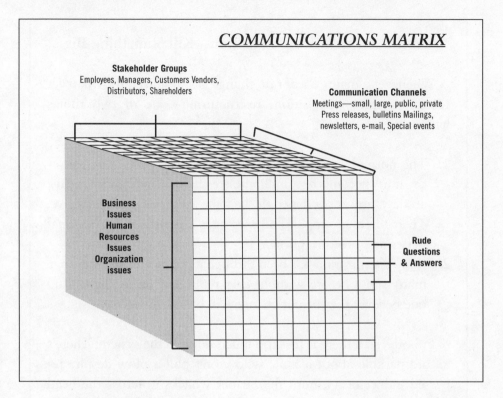

COMMUNICATIONS MATRIX

Stakeholder Groups
Employees, Managers, Customers Vendors, Distributors, Shareholders

Communication Channels
Meetings—small, large, public, private Press releases, bulletins Mailings, newsletters, e-mail, Special events

Business Issues Human Resources Issues Organization issues

Rude Questions & Answers

"What else?"

"Across the top of the matrix list all of the audiences that need to be informed: employees, managers, customers, suppliers, strategic business partners, investors, Wall Street analysts, the press, local municipal authorities, and so on. It will be a longer list than you initially expect it to be.

"Each issue and audience will intersect at a cell. Craft a short, simple position statement for each cell—twenty-five words or less that summarize the company's position on that issue relative to that audience. If an issue is irrelevant for a particular audience, that cell is crossed out. When each cell in the matrix has been filled, you will have a concise, authoritative guide to communicating consistent messages to all relevant constituencies. Done correctly, it will create more than awareness and understanding among the stakeholders. It will foster acceptance."

"But we don't have responses to all the issues yet. It'll take time to put together all the position statements. Some things will have to wait for the transition teams to make recommendations to the senior execs."

On the Art of Getting Attention—Kill Something Big

Whenever a major corporate change is announced for whatever reason—merger, acquisition, restructuring—one of two things happens:

1. The normal self-interest of employees and customers causes them to succumb to a million distractions. Uncertainty reigns, anxiety grows, and people become cautious and defensive. Their filters go up, and all messages are distilled by personal biases and preconceptions.
2. If the organization has been through announcements of change many times before without ever really having to change, no one believes the current change will be any different.

In both cases there is just too much noise in the system. There's an old parable about a mule who won't pull a plow despite repeated inducements, until the farmer whacks it across the head with a stout board. When an observer asks the farmer why he strikes the mule, the farmer replies that before he can get the mule to listen he has to get his attention.

In figurative terms, the same thing applies to people who have been numbed by news that may change their lives. Before you can effectively communicate with them, you have to get their attention.

The verbal equivalent to a whack on the side of the head is a two-part tactic: KSB—kill something big. First, announce something that shocks the workforce into attention, something that stimulates alert focus on your words—a major reallocation of resources that signals a shift in the business, substantial investment in a new technology, the formation or dissolution of a business unit.

Second, implement the change as rapidly as possible. The combination of a dramatic announcement and immediate execution demonstrates serious commitment and fosters awareness and ac-

ceptance unlike anything else. If the announcement and implementation is a growth initiative rather than a cost-cutting initiative, the
response will be more attentive and supportive and will probably
blunt any negative response to other cost-cutting initiatives.

You want to show people that you are serious, that this is the
time for giant steps, not incremental change. To accelerate through
a transition you need everyone's attention and acceptance of the
transition's inevitability.

Speed requires rapt attention to the message. Make sure they
hang on to your words. Kill something big. Get their attention.

*"That's not a problem. Start with what is known. The rule is to
communicate what you know, as soon as you know it. No secrets. No
surprises. No hype. No empty promises. Those are adults out there.
Treat them as intelligent individuals.*

*"If you hold out on them, they'll eventually figure it out, and they'll
start holding out on you. You'll lose whatever trust you've earned. If you
don't have an answer to everything yet, that's okay. Tell them you're working on the issues, so they know that you're aware of their concerns, that
somebody is worrying about them. That way they don't have to worry.
Oh, and by the way, communicate when there will be definitive answers."*

"So we just fill in the blanks with what we know?"

*"That's right, Andrew. It's very systematic and very comprehensive.
You avoid having a communications plan with holes in it. The point of
developing this matrix is to provide one-stop authority and consistency
on where the company stands on post-deal issues, from strategy to operations to human resources. But that's not all. There's a third dimension
to the matrix: communication channels—memos, face-to-face meetings,
small group sessions, press releases, newsletters, ads, commercials, TV
interviews, town hall meetings, and more.*

*"Andrew, during the transition messages will be sent through a vari-
ety of channels—the more channels, the better. People often interpret the
same message differently, depending on which channel delivers it to*

*them. If the company plans to outsource your department, for example,
you may well interpret the facts in different ways, depending on whether
you get the news from a friend, a supervisor, or a press release. Some
messages are better communicated to certain audiences through one
channel rather than another. Some should be communicated repeatedly
through all channels to reinforce the content again and again."*

"So it's a strategic decision."

*"That's right, but the bottom line is consistency in communication.
The company has to speak out of one side of its mouth. The matrix is a
map of reliable information in a time of rumor and confusion. It won't
prevent emotional wounds, of course, but timely communication of its
messages will help reduce turmoil, stabilize the company, strengthen
management's credibility, and build stakeholder acceptance."*

Enlisting Middle Management

Middle managers especially can be a prime source of disaffection.
They are rarely included in the decision to do the deal. They feel blindsided by the announcement and left out of important decisions. Worse
yet, in the early days after the announcement they rarely have any more
meaningful information than the rank-and-file employees.

When employees besiege their managers with questions, the managers feel foolish. They have no answers. No one wants to feel foolish. So
they become frustrated and angry. Not wanting to appear uninformed,
they tend to hide from the questioners, or even worse, to make up the answers. The result is wild inaccuracy, inconsistency, speculation, and resentment, forcing top management to reel from cri-
sis to crisis, trying to correct mis-perceptions, often too late.

To eliminate this problem, the communication matrix can be used for coaching and coun-

> **Middle managers especially can be a prime source of disaffection. They are rarely included in the decision to do the deal. They feel blindsided by the announcement and left out of important decisions. Worse yet, in the early days after the announcement they rarely have any more meaningful information than the rank-and-file employees.**

seling managers throughout the company. They can be briefed on stakeholder concerns, likely questions, and approved answers. The best approach to the briefing is to formulate a rude question for each stakeholder issue and craft a diplomatic answer. Since most managers become flustered by the rude questions often asked by impatient employees, agitated customers, demanding investors, and anxious suppliers, rude Q&As prepare them for the worst, build their confidence, and make them feel like insiders.

Many of the questions will not lend themselves to neat, simple, answers. Because of this there often is great temptation to explain why the question is complex and provide a rationale before any answer is given. To employees and other stakeholders this sounds like stalling. It lowers credibility and raises doubts about whatever answer finally is given. It is far better to answer the question as directly as possible first, and then follow with an explanation, than it is to do it the other way around. Same number of words. Much different result.

This communication coaching does wonders to garner the support of middle managers, who now feel informed and equipped to handle employee questions. They are given uniformly consistent answers to the most blunt employee questions. "How many people are you gonna let go?" "When are they going?" "What job will I get?" "Don't we get any training?" "What did you do to my health insurance?" "We're paid less than our counterparts in the other company—what are you gonna do about it?"

When questions can be answered truthfully—as middle managers can be trained to do—some of those fearsome snakes are being dealt with early. Identify the painful issues and get a clear, defensible company line on each issue in as few words as possible. Nothing is better for management's credibility than to respond to difficult questions as early as possible with direct, concise, honest answers, even when the answer is "We don't know, but we should be able to answer that question by. . ."

Remember the Customers

Needless to say, the same openness and honesty should be extended to paying customers. If it isn't, prepare to lose more value.

Anybody who monitered the 1996 takeover of First Interstate Bank by Wells Fargo knows the fun regional competitors had at Wells' expense. Institutions like Glendale Federal took out radio, billboard and print ads poking fun at the Wells leviathan and how it would roll over customers, reduce service, and increase fees. It was an unabashed strategy to steal depositors and key employees.

Glendale Federal radio spots featured lively ditties like the following "Cattle Song," written by April Winchell of Radio Savant and sung (with sound effects) to the tune of "Rawhide," the theme song of the Clint Eastwood television series by the same name:

> *"Merging, merging*
> *My old bank is merging*
> *And I'm going out of my mind.*
> *Every time I go there*
> *Things are really slow there*
> *Seems I'm always waiting in line.*
> *It's an uphill battle.*
> *They're treating me like cattle*
> *And they're simply wasting my time.*
> *If this is stagecoach banking,*
> *I'd rather have a spanking.*
> *I'm waiting, waiting, waiting in line.*
> *Move them in, hang around,*
> *Check your watch, get annoyed,*
> *Stand in line, check you nails look around, stand in line"*

The print ads (see pp. 85-86) showed Wells Fargo executives stepping on small businesses, raising rates, and shoving small business men off the Wells Stagecoach.

The campaign worked. After paying a 26 percent premium for First Interstate, Wells watched deposits evaporate and earnings slide. Wells, itself, is now being taken over.

Customers are often the most ignored when it comes to clear, non-hyped, post-deal communications. Hence, they are the first to heed your competitors,

Wells Fargo just got rid of their Intermediate Business Account, leaving small businesses in the dust. Buck 'em! And come over to Glendale Federal. We've got an account just like the one they canceled, only better. And, if you sign up by May 31, you'll get a year's worth of free checking and up to $100 worth of free checks. Call 1-800-FED UP.

Back in the Wild West, Wells Fargo branches were often the target for robbers. So maybe all the fees they're charging people today are their way of getting even. If that doesn't sound fair, come on over to Glendale Federal Bank. You'll find friendly tellers and personal service. If you want, we can even switch your account right over the phone. Call us at 1-800-41-FED UP.

Has Wells Fargo squashed the very business account you went to them for? And you in the process? Come to Glendale Federal Bank. You'll find our business accounts give you the services you want, without the excessive fees. Stop by your nearest branch and open a new Intermediate Business Checking Account by May 31 and we will give you one year's free checking and up to $100 worth of free checks. Or switch your account right over the phone by calling us at 1-800-41-FED UP.

> **If customers are not at the top of your priority list, redo the list. Customers are a precious asset, hard to gain and easy to lose. This is the time to court them like never before. It's tough to expand the customer base if old customers are being left behind.**

who inevitably launch a merciless campaign offering to rescue them from the agony that your transition will supposedly inflict upon them.

When Vtel Corporation and Compression Labs (CLI) merged in 1996, they were the number two and three players in the videoconferencing market. The combination of Vtel and CLI's cutting-edge technology, niche focus and established customer base was perceived by the market leader as a competitive threat. The market leader responded with a memo to its sales force, dubbing Vtel's deal a merger of two losers. The memo explained how to discourage potential Vtel customers by citing a standard litany of post-merger problems. Predictably, the memo fell into the hands of customers and found its way to Vtel.

Vtel avoided Wells Fargo's mistake and reaped a public relations coup by taking its case directly to the market. They held meetings throughout the United States for end users and distributors. They described how their advanced technology, improved functionality, and enhanced customer service capability would benefit end users and improve sales opportunities for distributors.

After each meeting, Vtel's communications consultants interviewed the participants to get their candid response to the message. The feedback was provided to Vtel senior management who continued to craft the message to increase its effectiveness. The outcome: Vtel retained and grew its customer base while earning the respect of the industry.

If customers are not at the top of your priority list, redo the list. Customers are a precious asset, hard to gain and easy to lose. This is the time to court them like never before. It's tough to expand the customer base if old customers are being left behind. According to the PricewaterhouseCoopers survey, companies that executed slow transitions reported more than twice as many difficulties communicating with customers. Why? Because the slow transition meant a delayed communications plan.

Effective transition communication, simply put, is the art of supplying honest answers to the hard questions that good people ask when they're in the dark and worried. It is about much more than all-out, backslapping, ego-boosting promotion of the deal. It's about mobilizing support, building acceptance, and removing uncertainty.

8

Five Frogs on a Log

Launching Transition Teams

Here's a child's riddle:

Five frogs are sitting on a log.
Four decide to jump off. How many are left?
Answer: Five.
Why?
Because deciding and doing are not the same thing.

Silly, you say, but companies often confuse deciding with doing. Good at deciding, they dither at doing, partly because the potential for failure is no longer academic. It's real. Fearful of making mistakes, they become fearful of execution (double entendre intended). The result is interminable meetings, excessively detailed analysis and glacial progress.

All transitions would be successful if there were one giant brain orchestrating the whole process—establishing priorities, allocating resources, coordinating activities, and ensuring timely completion of all objectives. But that's not reality. There are lots of individual brains with lots of ideas, egos, biases, and needs. Execution is always more difficult than it seems.

A Lesson from the National Football League

A reporter in the back of the room raised his hand. One of the ESPN audio technicians jockeyed into position and handed the wireless microphone to the well-known reporter from the Tribune.

"Coach, your team entered this game as an overwhelming favorite, you had an extra week to prepare, and all your key players were healthy. So what do you think went wrong?"

The coach knew this would be the first question. He looked down at the base of the microphone, took a deep breath, and said what hundreds of coaches before him had said, and what hundreds of coaches after him would say: "We didn't execute. We had a good game strategy. Everybody on our team was ready to play. But we just plain didn't execute our game plan. We took bad penalties. We dropped too many balls. Twice we fumbled deep in our own zone. Too many guys tried to win the game on their own. Plain and simple, we lost our composure."

How many brutally honest CEOs, when asked to explain a failed merger or acquisition, would say almost the same thing? "We had a clear strategy, the necessary financial resources, a strong reputation, leading technology, and talented people. But we didn't execute. We lost too many key customers. We were late getting the new products to the market. We got distracted by transition activities and let our service levels slip. We just plain didn't execute our plans."

Whether it's a 350-pound offensive tackle bearing down on you with the single-minded intention of planting you in terra firma or a ruthless competitor willing to slash prices, trash your reputation, and steal your people to drive you into bankruptcy, the effect is the same. There is a natural and often overwhelming tendency to panic.

More postmortems have attributed failure to poor execution than any other cause. There are two reasons. First, many executives simply take execution for granted. Once the tough decisions are made, implementation is up to subordinates. In the minds of these executives, deciding really is doing. Filled with confidence and optimism after closing a deal, they say, "Hey, this is a no-brainer. Let's just form a bunch of transition teams and start working."

The second reason is that they fail to anticipate the complexity of large-scale change. In the flood of distractions and disruptions that accompanies mergers and acquisitions, for example, things can quickly spin out of control. Without a thoughtful, comprehensive, and well-rehearsed operational plan, managers get rattled, take their eye off objectives, become overwhelmed, and lose their composure.

Whether it's a 350-pound offensive tackle bearing down on you with the single-minded intention of planting you in terra firma or a ruthless competitor willing to slash prices, trash your reputation, and steal your people to drive you into bankruptcy, the effect is the same. There is a natural and often overwhelming tendency to panic. The result: chaos, confusion, and mayhem on your side of the line. Good for the other guys. Bad for you.

This is the scenario. The announcement of an acquisition or a major change is like a starting pistol being fired. The runners leave the blocks, but unlike a normal race everyone heads in their own direction scrambling to add value. With the best of intentions and a pinch of self-interest, line and staff managers alike race for an opportunity to influence the future.

They schedule planning meetings, contact counterparts in the other company, request information, send information, invite themselves to meetings, request that other managers attend their meetings, sketch new division and departmental structures, sort out transitional and permanent staffing issues, and adjust incentive structures to reflect new realities. They debate the integration of information and communication systems, argue about the speed and extent of consolidation, question cost-cutting and revenue enhancement assumptions, and scramble to

> **Customers feel the effects first. . . . They don't care about your internal problems, and they most certainly aren't going to pay you to fix them.**

hang on to and motivate key employees. The volume of additional work becomes overwhelming, and they cling to the belief that somehow more meetings will help them manage it.

When management's attention is being pulled in every conceivable direction, minor, quickly corrected distractions become a welcome relief. Managers begin to seek out the comfort of familiar crises—daily emergencies, minor oversights, and operational minutiae better left to subordinates. Unfortunately, these distractions take up time. Transition schedules slip. They fall behind.

Why would they allow themselves to be sucked into dithering when so many serious matters need to be resolved quickly? Because, in the midst of the transition turmoil, the quick resolution of minor issues gives them a sense of accomplishment, of being in control, if only momentarily. Instead of focusing on the real value drivers, they allow themselves to become mired in internal matters. This behavior wastes time, consumes valuable resources, and contributes little to value creation.

When execution breaks down, customers feel the effects first. They get less attention—shipments, service, and quality all start to slip through the cracks. Appointments are missed, messages get lost, and phones ring off the hooks. The last excuse they want to hear is that the problem is your post-deal transition. They don't care about your internal problems, and they most certainly aren't going to pay you to fix them.

When Planning Fails—The Two Extremes

Planning is the average manager's intuitive response to avoiding breakdowns in execution. But planning, too, can be executed poorly. In an attempt to combat chaos, bring order, provide clear direction, and get something done, companies tend to gravitate toward one of two planning extremes. They form too many transition teams and end up cre-

> There's an old yachtsman's creed: If you can't tie good knots, tie a lot of them. Many companies think that this applies to selecting transition teams.

ating a planning circus, or they scrupulously avoid anything resembling a participative process and end up creating a small "members-only" club.

The Planning Circus

There's an old yachtsman's creed: If you can't tie good knots, tie a lot of them. Many companies think that this applies to selecting transition teams.

In well-meaning attempts to smooth the way and broaden the sense of ownership, executives form dozens of teams composed of managers and other key contributors from each company to coordinate scores of post-deal decisions and activities. The teams usually are constructed to reflect functional areas of the organization. The mandate, when there is one, is to plan the transition and integration process, which generally includes developing recommendations for combining functions, systems, technologies, and intellectual capital, capturing scale economies, rethinking product and market strategies, and so on.

The basic idea is sound, but more often than not this method of promoting teamwork simply adds work and further prolongs the transition. In other words, it becomes a planning circus.

This is exactly what happened at a large regional bank. In a misguided notion of post-merger democracy, it established

> **It is not unusual for companies to rush off and build a byzantine structure of transition teams that superimposes its own mass, complexity, and inertia on the transition. The result is always suboptimal. Size slows speed and dilutes accountability.**

a seventeen-member executive transition team. This group oversaw twenty-four functional teams averaging nine managers per team, forty-eight subfunctional teams averaging six managers per team, and eight cross-functional teams with twelve managers per team. After subtracting overlaps, nearly five hundred managers were involved!

The teams met over a ten-month period after the deal. The opportunity cost, productivity losses, delays, and sheer expense of coordination escalated operating costs, stalled consolidation, and fueled confusion that spilled over to the customers. A year after the deal was announced the two companies still had not merged operations, much less captured any of the value that the deal was engineered to create. They had, however, managed to lose depositors and tarnish their reputation.

It is not unusual for companies to rush off and build a byzantine structure of transition teams that superimposes its own mass, complexity, and inertia on the transition. The result is always suboptimal. Size slows speed and dilutes accountability.

Another prime example occurred a few years back with the $8.3 billion merger of SmithKline Beckman and Beecham PLC, a union designed to gain economies rapidly by combining R&D operations for quicker and more prolific delivery of new drug products. But the merger turned into a highly publicized example of a convoluted and extended transition that saw operating costs, debt, and interest expense rise while R&D synergy faltered amid a hierarchy of 250 transition teams. The irony was that eighteen months after the deal was done, the companies had yet to take the first step toward combining R&D. They were still slogging through endless transition team meetings!

> **There is a difference between an agile fleet of teams and a bloated armada.**

Unfortunately, this lesson was not learned by other pharmaceutical and chemical company giants merging today. In the midst of growing competition and rapid industry consolidation, some of SmithKline Beecham's competitors are emulating its transition practices and creating vast armies of multitiered, multinational transition teams. They fail to grasp that there is a difference between an agile fleet of teams and a bloated armada.

A Members-Only Club

The other transition team extreme is to create a small, exclusive, secretive club of executives who make all the decisions, plan all the action, and then tell everybody what to do. Pursuing this path can stall cooperative decision making and ultimately have the same suboptimal effect as

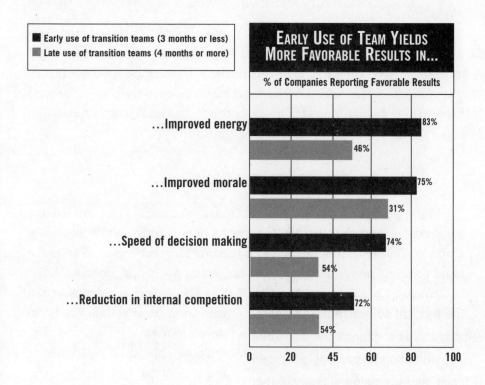

having too many teams. Witness Tonka Corporation's acquisition of the well-regarded, but underperforming, Kenner toy and Parker game businesses some years ago.

Unwilling to convene transition teams to focus quickly on the opportunities in the merger, Tonka's CEO vested all transition decision making in a small group of senior executives focused entirely on the performance of their own fiefdoms, despite the fact that significant product line, development, sales channel, and infrastructure consolidations were among the deal's justifications. Prolonged indecision on these matters, as well as on organization structure, management deployment, and business strategy, caused Tonka to founder and left it frantically searching for a hit toy that would cover up the company's poor integration and lack of resolution on so many issues. Unable to compete successfully on its own, Tonka eventually was swallowed up by Hasbro.

The Upside of Transition Teams

The hazards of using transition teams should not dissuade a company altogether from taking a team-based approach to accelerating a transition. According to the results of the PricewaterhouseCoopers survey, companies that utilized transition teams early in the change process experienced higher morale, more enthusiasm, and speedier decision making—all crucial to an accelerated transition.

Scripting Early Moves

Many argue that the purpose of transition teams is to complete the hundreds of tasks that surface as part of a major transition. While this is a potential benefit, it is not the real reason. The real reason is to make rapid progress on things that create real economic value, real fast.

The tactical objective of the transition teams is to launch the transition with such force, single-minded focus, and precision movement that no competitor, critic, cynic, or skeptic can knock it off course.

The primary purpose of a transition team should not be to develop or validate strategy. The purpose should be to accelerate implementation of strategy. The process of forming and chartering these teams is aimed at defining concrete deliverables, creating clearly defined roles, and committing the organization to specific timetables for taking action. The process for launching the teams is aimed at raising the energy level high enough so that the teams will demolish any obstacle, while keeping them composed enough not to make dumb mistakes.

Well-focused transition teams are the fuse that ignites an accelerated transition. In the middle of chaos and confusion, using teamwork, discipline, and precision, execution is the only strategy that really works.

The tactical objective of the transition teams is to launch the transition with such force, single-minded focus, and precision movement that no competitor, critic, cynic, or skeptic can knock it off course.

Pitfalls and Prescriptions

Pitfall: Most companies create too many teams.

The tendency among consultants is to recommend transition teams for every function, business unit, and geographical division, as well as cross-functional teams for key products, services, and system integration.

More is not better. Too many teams means too many people doing too many things and at too great a cost in productivity, opportunity, and general disruption.

Prescription: Group the value drivers into categories to determine how many teams you realistically need.

There should always be fewer teams than value drivers.

Another Lesson from the NFL

The San Fransisco Forty-Niners, one of the most successful football teams in the NFL, adopted a derivation of this strategy and used it to help win five Super Bowl victories. Fully aware of the extraordinarily high levels of energy and excitement exhibited at the beginning of a football game, and knowing how important it is for the offense to execute flawlessly, they decided to script out and practice their first few dozen plays. Rather than call the plays from the sideline and risk mistakes and confusion during the highly emotional early stages of a game, they studied the opposition in advance, decided on a game plan, and then scripted out the first few series of plays. Then, in practice, they drilled in the formations, snap counts, pass patterns, and blocking schemes.

As most football fans know, the defensive team is at its fastest, fiercest, and most aggressive during the beginning of the game. This can be more than a little distracting to the offensive team, which usually depends on cool, calm, precision timing in order to execute its offensive game plan. Having scripted and well-rehearsed plays already in mind prevents the very high level of emotion at the start of a game from interfering with the offense's ability to perform. The behaviors drilled in during practice take over. The result is fewer mistakes, higher efficiency, and greater production.

In essence, this is the same strategy that works for launching transition teams. Decide on the game plan (the value drivers) and script the plays (transition team action plans).

If you accept the proposition that the real value of transition teams is to launch the transition with force, single-minded focus, and precision movement, then it should be clear that a few small, fast-paced teams, following a disciplined process, are best. If you don't accept this proposition, skip the rest of this chapter.

Pitfalls and Prescriptions

Pitfall: Most companies put too many people on each transition team.

At companies with transition teams of ten to twelve people each, which is not uncommon, just scheduling a meeting becomes a nightmare because of calendar conflicts. Worse yet, twelve people can't make a timely decision, and nothing gets done because everyone assumes someone else is doing it.

Some companies have a culture in which it's standard to have twelve, fifteen, or even twenty or more people in a meeting. At most public utilities, for example, you'll find two dozen people in a meeting when only four of them really need to be there.

Bottom line: Not much gets done. The entire transition gets extended.

Prescription: Keep transition teams small.

Get them down to three to five people. Besides allowing earlier and more rapid scheduling of meetings and milestones, fewer people per team clarifies accountability: it becomes obvious if someone isn't pulling his or her weight or delivering in a timely manner.

Pitfalls and Prescriptions

Pitfall: Teams have too much autonomy.

After transition teams are configured and convened, senior executives often pay little attention to them until the first status reports are given. Although autonomy is valued by most professionals, it is problematic for transition teams and raises several concerns.

The first concern is executive ownership of the transition teams' recommendations. Transition teams often find that the assumptions that drove the deal and figured significantly into the price are inaccurate or invalid, or that the costs of capturing savings are well in excess of what was expected. If a transition team has been operating autonomously, executives will be blindsided by these revelations and will fail to understand and appreciate the care with which they were investigated.

A second concern is how to keep transition teams aligned with the economic value drivers in the deal. Teams often become so involved in their assignments that they lose focus on the value drivers. Without oversight, they may not realize they have drifted before valuable time has been lost.

A third concern is that autonomous teams are not as willing as they should be to share data in a timely manner. Neither do they consolidate their requests for information, thereby placing a burden on other information providers.

Prescription: Each transition team should be sponsored by a member of the executive team.

The sponsor need not be involved in each meeting or deliverable, but he or she should be kept informed of progress and results and considered a member of the team. The sponsorship solution secures executive ownership of the results, reduces the potential for an adversarial debate over unexpected findings, maintains alignment with the economic value drivers, and encourages interteam cooperation and the sharing of data and analysis.

Pitfalls and Prescriptions

Pitfall: The launch comes too late.

When a merger or acquisition is announced, it can be months before the deal is actually closed—sometimes a few months, sometimes as long as a year in the case of public utilities. All too often the company waits until after the deal is closed or until federal regulatory reviews are completed before it forms and launches transition teams. Employees usually are told not to say or do anything until the papers are signed, for fear of wrecking the deal or potentially violating federal restrictions on the sharing of competitive data. This means there will be no viable plans for day one.

Prescription: Launch teams as soon as possible.

The Hart-Scott-Rodino Act does not prohibit basic planning for execution of the transition. It places constraints only on the kind of data that are shared between companies, what is communicated, and what the companies can do jointly prior to approval. As long as companies respect the constraints and avoid "jumping the gun" a regulatory approved basic planning can begin with the announcement. If a transition team requires prohibited data for its planning prior to federal approval, the companies can give the data to an independent third party who can conduct a confidential analysis, aggregate the results, and communicate an allowable summary of the findings, thereby enabling the transition teams to move ahead with their planning.

The transition teams should be formed as soon after the announcement as possible—contingent, of course, on completion of the value driver analysis. This will help to ensure a plan for day one and facilitate early decision-making and implementation.

Selecting Transition Teams

Configuration of transition teams should take place after the value drivers have been prioritized. This is both a natural and efficient point at which to begin clustering the value drivers and identifying the number of teams and the membership needed to accelerate implementation.

This is not the time to engage in representational democracy. The primary reason for a transition team is to execute rapidly on the 20 percent of value drivers that will drive 80 percent of the economic value with the highest probability of success. Creating additional transition teams or expanding the size of each team simply to achieve balance between merger partners or to avoid hurting someone's feelings will quickly lead to a planning circus.

There is sometimes a desire to create additional teams around the hundreds of administrative tasks that do not fall into the value driver category but must be done regardless. To ensure timeliness, these tasks are best delegated to responsible individuals within the functions, rather than to teams.

Inevitably, there are certain value drivers, like systems integration and data conversion, that, owing to time and cost requirements, tend not to fall in the targeted 20 percent of value drivers. These drivers are "table stakes"—critical to the success of other drivers, they are often very complex and costly. It is appropriate to select a transition for these value drivers.

A transition team should be selected for each cluster of value drivers. Configuring teams on the basis of functional knowledge (for example, sales and marketing), line of business, special initiative, or market segment is common. But cross-functional teams are not unusual for complex value drivers. There is no right number, rule of thumb, or formula. It is best to select the fewest number of teams possible without overburdening any one team with too many value drivers.

Staffing the Teams

This is where incremental economic value creation begins. Therefore, transition teams should be staffed with the best and the brightest people in the organization. To whatever extent possible, team members should be both the behavioral role models and the leaders of the future. The opportunity afforded participants to influence important business decisions not only provides added psychic rewards but helps offset the perceived loss of impact that accompanies a transition. This tactic also helps retain key individual and managerial contributors.

Often large companies, notably utilities and insurance companies with large numbers of administrative staff and large health care organizations with a pathological need to include everyone, attempt to populate the transition teams primarily with staff managers. Avoid any such temptation. The usual reason given is to keep line managers focused on operations, customers, and the marketplace. However, when staff managers are in the majority, they tend to turn transition teams into careers and slow the process.

Teams should have three to five members, including the captain—any more and they cannot coordinate their calendars to schedule their meetings. The specific assignment of an individual to a team should be guided more by the expertise required to implement the value drivers than an effort to mix the merged companies' managers, build cross-functional appreciation, or foster teamwork.

Representational democracy, horse-trading, and ego-boosting have no place in the transition process. These transition teams are small, focused, and under intense pressure to perform. People without the knowledge, skills, or abilities to contribute in meaningful ways don't belong on a transition team.

Team captains should be selected in advance by the executive team. Asking a team to elect its own captain when it meets to begin work is generally a mistake. (Would a professional football team elect the quarterback when they huddled up?)

There should also be a small executive team accountable for the end result of the transition. Each member of the executive team should be assigned as the sponsor of one or more transition teams. The role of the sponsor is to coach the team without doing the work of the team. This person is accountable for ensuring that the team stays on track, doesn't lose sight of the main objective, and has the resources and information needed to complete its assignments. When issues arise that intersect with other team assign-

> Representational democracy, horse-trading, and ego-boosting have no place in the transition process. These transition teams are small, focused, and under intense pressure to perform. People without the knowledge, skills, or abilities to contribute in meaningful ways don't belong on a transition team.

ments or require senior management action or decision, the sponsor provides support.

As a member of top management, the sponsor has the positional power to run interference for the team and resolve problems caused by cross-team interdependencies. For example, in one merger the marketing team and the operations team required significant information technology resources to integrate critical systems (the sales order processing system and the production tracking system). The executive sponsor took the issue to the senior management team to determine which team's needs should receive priority. As it turned out, the marketing team's needs were met first, but only for a critical module. The operations team was authorized to proceed after the close of the deal by using the acquired company's tracking system for the first two quarters of the year.

Launching the Transition

There are three objectives for the launch phase:
1. Create a common understanding of the reasons for the transition, the value drivers, and the actions that must be taken over the next few months to accelerate progress.
2. Create concrete action plans for each value driver.
3. Energize the teams to act.

In football parlance, it's called scripting the plays and motivating the team before it goes onto the playing field.

The most efficient and effective process is to conduct a two-day off-site launch of all the transition teams simultaneously. Meetings held on-site invariably get interrupted. Every time a team member or executive gets called out for something else, the team starts circling. A two-day off-site

> **In football parlance, it's called scripting the plays and motivating the team before it goes onto the playing field.**

accomplishes about as much as a weeklong on-site meeting.

If the launch is for a merger, the session usually begins with the

CEOs of the two companies offering brief company histories punctuated by stories and photos of humorous events. If done well, this opener takes some of the edginess out of the event and helps the participants get comfortable. It also sets the stage for understanding the value in the deal.

The opener is followed by a concise statement about why the deal is being done—the business opportunity and the value to be extracted. This is followed by a review of the value drivers and the process by which they were identified. A question-and-answer session is then followed by a step-by-step review of what is expected from the transition teams over the next two days and thereafter.

Team members and captains are announced, and the working agendas are issued. Teams then meet to begin an expedited planning process that produces detailed action plans for their assigned value drivers. Throughout the two days, the teams reconvene at various points to share progress, surface concerns, address cross-team dependencies, identify issues to be resolved by the executive team, and critically review their evolving action plans. All the teams assemble at the end to present plans to the group, solicit feedback, make adjustments, and commit to time schedules.

Immediately following the launch, all the plans are consolidated into a master transition schedule. Since much of the work of the teams will occur in the weeks following the meeting, an executive supported by a staff member is usually assigned to monitor progress on behalf of the entire organization.

Unlike traditional management planning retreats, these transition team launch sessions possess an urgency and task orientation that sets them apart. The teams follow very prescribed agendas, with clearly defined output requirements. Also, these sessions act to excite and energize the new team of executives in a way that traditional sessions do not.

> **Unlike traditional management planning retreats, these transition team launch sessions possess an urgency and task orientation that sets them apart.**

The simple act of crowding everyone into one place serves to motivate them to push one another to achieve the goal. Psychologists call it social facilitation. A whole group of peers simultaneously performing gives everyone the sense of being onstage; everyone feels pressure to contribute. Adrenaline flows. People anticipate being part of something important, meaningful, and dramatic.

The Postseason

Unlike professional sports teams, companies undergoing major change don't really have a postseason. The transition teams complete their missions and then disband. The hard work and disciplined approach used at the launch and throughout the transition often become part of the way managers make decisions and take action long into the future.

But something else has usually occurred. These new leaders have been part of a defining moment in the life of their organization. They have been present at the birth of a new company or a new way of doing things. Not the cork-popping, champagne-toasting close of a big deal, but the point at which a new group of leaders came together for the first time, in a strange hotel, with ugly decor and bad food, and launched the future. They were there.

9

Acute Structural Anxiety

Organization Structure and Role Clarity

Mergers, acquisitions, and other large-scale changes are case studies in organizational uncertainty. Seldom do executives experience more intense pressure to clarify authority, establish control, and solidify reporting relationships than they do in the period immediately following the launch of a major transition. If there were a formal psychiatric term for this condition, it would probably be "acute structural anxiety syndrome."

The CEO is usually the first to be afflicted with acute structural anxiety, and the side effects are particularly destructive to a company. This syndrome induces decisions that favor form over function, titles over accountability, and hierarchy over role clarity. In mergers and acquisitions, the first symptoms appear during the horse-trading and negotiating that accompany the earliest stages of a transition,

> **Bridgestone learned about delay the hard way when it acquired Firestone. "Rather than aggressively merging the two companies [Bridgestone] kept Firestone's sales and marketing operations separate from [its own], thus losing many of the cost advantages of the deal and fostering competition between the two arms."**
>
> *Martin Dickson*, Financial Times *(August 24, 1993)*

and it manifests itself as an obsessive preoccupation with publishing an organization chart.

The merger and acquisition discussions begin around issues of growth, market share, and strategic advantage but quickly deteriorate into a struggle for power, authority, and turf. Who is going to be in charge of what? ("I'll be chairman for three years, you be CEO.") Will I report to her, or will she report to me? ("When I retire, you can become chairman and restructure the executive team.") Will I have the same level of authority and influence? Will I have a bigger or smaller job? Will my people feel that I took care of them? ("Pick your own chief operating officer, but let's keep my chief financial officer and VP of sales. I don't much care who we pick for HR.") These concerns lead to early compromises and commitments that encumber the new structure.

Outside the context of negotiation, such structural compromises are indefensible. They bear little relation to the creation of shareholder value and often lead to conflicting business models. The new leadership begins with a handicap—the hand that was dealt them.

Furthermore, these accommodations ripple through the organization. In a misguided attempt to balance the bartering at the executive level, mid- and lower-level managers are often selected for inappropriate jobs. The result is an organization that serves politics at the expense of performance and personalities at the expense of productivity.

Acute structural anxiety syndrome is often the cause when CEOs adopt another dangerous tactic: delay. In an effort to minimize disruptions, they simply put off making any organizational changes at all. The logic behind delay is that people need time to "get used to the idea of working together."

Instead of helping people get used to working together, the uncertainty caused by delay paralyzes managers who fear for their future and distracts already uneasy employees from the job at hand. The result is a game of musical chairs. Executives begin jockeying for a position even before the music starts. Worst of all, the speed, focus, and early momentum necessary to achieving the accelerated transition are sacrificed at the altar of corporate politics.

Clearly this is not the way to organize a successful business. Struc-

Three Popular Snake-Oil Remedies for Acute Structural Anxiety Syndrome

Remedy 1: The Replication Solution

1. Make up a list of all the other companies you want to emulate, maybe those that have appeared in recent issues of *Fortune* or *Forbes* or in Tom Peters and Robert H. Waterman's book *In Search of Excellence.*
2. Copy their organization charts.
3. Select the chart that has the same number of executive boxes as you have executives.
4. Customize the titles to reflect the ego needs of your management team.

Remedy 2: The Assimilation Solution

1. Superimpose your organization chart over the acquired company's organization chart.
2. Assimilate any unique elements into your structure.
3. Inform critics that resistance is futile.

Remedy 3: The Accommodation Solution

1. Count the number of executives in each organization.
2. Design a chart to accommodate all of those who have not elected early retirement.
3. Introduce the new structure as a "paradigm shift in executive teaming."

Like an elixir from the traveling medicine man, these unsophisticated cures often do more harm than good. They encourage power grabbing and turn well-meaning attempts to clarify roles into hollow promises. That's because the structures are generated in a vacuum and do not relate to the business value drivers that propelled the changes taking place.

tural decisions have profound implications for the productivity and performance of the new organization. The impact extends well beyond
charts, layers, and headcounts. It leads to the breakup or alteration of
existing work groups, the creation of new work groups, changes in work
flow and decision flow, alteration of individual roles and accountabilities, and modification of the superior-subordinate status of individuals.
It has an overwhelming effect on behavior, motivation, and the ultimate
capture of shareholder value.

Unfortunately, the push for a table of organization is the first and
last refuge of structurally challenged executives. They believe the chart is
the organization. For example:

CEO: *"So just exactly what should we do?"* shouted the CEO, *frustrated with one of the most counterintuitive pieces of advice he had ever received.*

Advisor: *"Don't publish an organization chart."*

CEO: *"Why not?"*

Advisor: *"Because it's only going to provide half of an answer and you will frustrate the people even more."*

CEO: *"What do you mean, half an answer?"*

Advisor: *"People want to know more than who they report to. They want to know what is expected of them, what they are answerable for, what decisions they own, and what decisions they share. Boxes and lines don't answer these questions."*

CEO: *"But how will they know who they report to?"*

Advisor: *"Tell them."*

CEO: *"I still think we need a chart!"*

Advisor: "It's your company."

Five days later, the CEO publishes an organization chart. Now the entire organization is saying: "So what does this mean?" For example:

"Hey, his job looks like it's a more important job than mine. But we started at the same time and he does the same things." (Explanation: the box for his job was inadvertently drawn higher on the chart.)

"How does my job in California relate to that guy in New York? It looks like he has the same job, but he reports at a higher level. Who's doing what around here? I wonder what he gets paid?"

"Where's the P&L responsibility? We can't both have it?"

"I refuse to report to someone who has been given the senior-level position simply as a convenience to the CEO. They're afraid he'll split and take his accounts. Who owns the accounts? Him or the company? Apparently they're not afraid of losing the people who report to him. Is he going to have complete authority over what I do?"

CEO: "Nobody gets it. Nobody is happy. I thought this would answer their questions!"

Advisor: "It's only a chart, it raises as many questions as it attempts to answer. You still need to define roles."

CEO: "How?"

Advisor: "Start with the value drivers. Define the impact that each executive position has on driving value in the new organization. Then describe the results for which each executive position is accountable, what decisions each position owns, which decisions each position shares, and the interdependencies between all of the executive positions. Then do the same thing for subordinates. The resulting set of accountabilities and interdependencies will define a detailed structure that supports the business strategy. Then *the organization chart can be drawn."*

Today's organizations have been built on yesterday's experience. The new organizations need to be built around tomorrow's challenges. And these new challenges present greater complexity and demand more interconnectivity. Complex roles and interrelationships are not clarified by publishing an organization chart.

Organization charts communicate more about authority, status, power, and turf than about how information should flow and how decisions should be made. Clearly everyone needs to know to whom they report. But knowing reporting relationships does not ensure productivity and high performance.

High performance is a byproduct of organizational clarity. Clarity about how a person influences end results and what that person's role is in relationship to the roles of others. "In the new structure, do I make the decision about hiring the field sales managers, or do I need to get the product manager's agreement?" "In this new matrix organization, who makes incentive payout recommendations? Who approves them?" "Since we need to change our distributor agreements, what is my role in cutting these deals?"

These are the kinds of questions that managers often raise but seldom are answered by an organization chart. Until individual roles relative to core processes are addressed, the only value of an organization chart is to provide senior executives with a superficial sense of control.

> **Good organizational design is about the optimization of performance, not the accommodation of ego.**

Organizational compromises totally unrelated to the value drivers begin to surface early. To accommodate and preserve roles for middle managers with deep knowledge of the business, integrated business units are disintegrated to increase the number of positions. New functions are created, and the organization becomes more fragmented. Employees quickly become confused about who does what and why. This increases the urgency to publish an organization chart.

Unfortunately, publishing an organization chart provides only half an answer. People want to know what is expected of them, what they are accountable for, and what decisions they own. Boxes and lines don't answer these questions, and half an answer only heightens confusion and exasperation. Changing roles and complex interrelationships are not clarified with the publication of a traditional organization chart.

An organization's structure ought to provide support for execution, not simply clarify hierarchy. Good organization design communicates a framework for execution and serves, first and foremost, the business's basic value proposition. It enables achievement of value-driving initiatives. Role clarity is achieved only when each manager's impact on the value drivers is clearly defined.

This is not to say that you should not publish a chart of reporting lines. Rather, you should not expect effective execution until you can also publish the accountability (answerability for end results) and decision authority for each position on the chart and define how the configuration supports the creation of long-term, sustained economic value. The organization chart must be a structural map that clarifies roles and interdependencies around key results that support implementation of the company's business strategy.

> **You can no more create role clarity by drawing an organization chart than you can make it rain by washing your car.**
>
> *Fred Grauer, co-chairman of Barclays Global Investors*

Consider the following: A leading basic-metals manufacturer acquired its major distributor. Two different sales forces with different operating styles now had to work together to service overlapping accounts. The acquiring company possessed metals manufacturing strengths, including product quality, technical support, and new product development. The distributor was recognized for its fast turnaround times, service, flexibility, competitive prices, knowledge of customer needs, and product quality. Thirty-five percent of the new company's sales volume would be derived from common accounts.

One of the value drivers involved rapidly defining how common ac-

ACCOUNTABILITIES AND KEY DECISIONS

	1	2	3	4	5	6	7
Manufacturer:							
Sales representative	P*+	P+	S		S*	C	C
Sales office administrator	C	C	C			P	
Product manager	S	C					
Marketing specialist	C	S*	C			C	
Scheduler			C	C	S*		
Production manager						C	
Engineer						S	S*
Metallurgist						C	
Credit specialist				C			
Acquired Distributor:							
Outside sales rep.	P+	P*+	S		S	S	C
Inside sales rep.		C	C	C	C	C	C
Plant manager		C	C	S	C		
Materials manager		C	C	S			
Metallurgist					S	S	
Credit specialist						C	

ABBREVIATIONS: *P= Primary accountability; S = Shared accountability with specific other(s); C = Contributory accountability (provide advice and counsel);* * = *Lead;* + = *Specific accounts.*

END RESULT KEY: *1 – Pricing; 2 – Quoting Delivery 3 – Resolving Nontechnical Problems; 4 – Scheduling Orders in the Factory; 5 – Resolving Technical Problems; 6 – Providing Technical Support; 7 – Providing Administrative Support.*

counts would be managed. It wasn't just a matter of heaving these accounts into one sales organization or the other. Success depended on clearly defining each manager's role in the new organization. With a few hours of work, management was able to map roles and interrelationships for managing shared accounts.

In this case, there was no need to change reporting relationships. But without clarity as to how the pricing and discounting decisions, selling tactics, account management, service requirements, and so

---

Functional Fixity

Many years ago a German psychologist gave two groups of people identical collections of odds and ends: a cardboard box, a candle, matches, an eyedropper, a role of tape, a washer, a pencil, several thumbtacks, a thimble, and some coins. Each person was told to mount the candles on a nearby wall, using any of the objects at hand. More than twice as many people in one group succeeded than in the other group.

One group was filled with geniuses and the other with dimwits, right? Not at all. The solution involved melting wax onto the box, sticking the candle into the wax, and then tacking the cardboard box, with the candle attached, to the wall with the thumbtacks. The poor showing from the people in one group came down to one vital difference: the candles were placed in the cardboard boxes before they were given to this group, whereas for the other group the objects and the box were simply laid out on a table.

The people in the first group were more likely than those in the second group to perceive the boxes as containers, not as supports or shelves.

People in organizations are often perceived like those cardboard boxes. Because they serve in a particular role, their contributions are presumed to be limited to that role. Executives who can't learn to see people outside of their functional boxes will continue to encounter self-imposed barriers to innovation.

on, were to be handled by the two organizations, chaos would have resulted.

This map became the equivalent of a pattern on the floor for a complex dance step that had to be performed flawlessly in front of customers. The most compelling outcome, though, was not a well-diagrammed tango, but rather the collective epiphany of the two companies' managers when they finished mapping roles relative to this value driver.

The utility of this technique is not limited to mergers and acquisitions. It can add value in any environment where roles are changing, interrelationships are complex, and the delineation of personal impact on the value drivers is what separates clarity from confusion, order from chaos, and winners from losers.

This approach is not bound by traditional roles. An important marketing initiative is just as likely to be driven by an operations manager as by a product manager, because responsibilities are defined around the skills and capabilities of key managers rather than stereotypic roles.

By overcoming this form of functional fixity—solving the problem outside the restrictive boxes of a traditional organization chart—this company unleashed the latent creative and productive capacity of the organization. Executives challenged to manage outside their comfort zones of functional knowledge were forced to rely on critical and conceptual thinking skills—exactly the kind of thinking needed to design innovative solutions in an increasingly competitive world. Though increased innovation is not generally a primary structural objective, it becomes an important, positive side effect.

Organizations that demand procedural compliance suffer from creative constipation. They turn bureaucrats into heroes, reward diligence with delay, sand the sharp edges off of good ideas, and demoralize optimists. Ultimately, they evolve into parasitic organisms that suck shareholder value into a black hole of infrastructure. No light can escape.

Organizations that fail to establish this role clarity relative to value drivers experience higher levels of confusion and resistance, as well as an escalated need for coordination and control. They respond by proliferating controls that burden staff with excessive policies.

Organizations that demand procedural compliance suffer from creative constipation. They turn bureaucrats into heroes, reward diligence with delay, sand the sharp edges off of good ideas, and demoralize optimists. Ultimately, they evolve into parasitic organisms that suck shareholder value into a black hole of infrastructure. No light can escape.

10

The Two-and-a-Half-Ton Truck

Policies and Practices

In wartime, army supply battalions are required to move supply depots to maintain proximity with fighting units. Protecting and accounting for the inventory of expensive equipment and supplies when under constant assault by scavengers, impatient officers, and black marketers is a constant challenge. Supply officers are held to account and often called on the carpet for even minor discrepancies in inventory.

A former colleague who served in the Vietnam War recalled that a typical practice was to load several dozen large trucks and travel in a convoy to the next supply point. On one of these moves, a two-and-a-half-ton truck blew out a tire while ascending a narrow, winding road in a treacherous canyon. The driver jumped to safety before the truck slid over the edge and tumbled several hundred feet, exploding in a fireball at the bottom of the canyon.

The officer in charge, having witnessed the entire event, turned to the supply sergeant and said, "Sergeant, everything missing from inventory since my arrival—every missing canister, lost piece of equipment, and unaccounted-for supply unit—was on that truck. Understood?" The sergeant smiled and replied, "Yes, sir, a real tragedy."

One of the unstated advantages of a merger or acquisition is the opportunity it affords a business to renovate outdated structures and align new roles with business priorities. A merger provides a temporary shield for altering structure, redeploying people, redesigning roles, and reconfiguring core work processes and systems.

When companies convoy to their next spot on the competitive landscape, the transition provides a unique opportunity to pack every broken policy, grandfathered program, and boondoggled practice onto a policy truck and push it over the side of a cliff. During a merger everyone expects sweeping change and the elimination of some practices and processes along the way. There will never be a better excuse (short of a financial disaster) for discarding policies that are not adding value.

Unfortunately, this opportunity to dynamite practices and processes that constrain and obstruct performance is typically lost in a narrow-minded, post-deal rush to reduce cost. Management teams begin carving out costs before fixing or even understanding the systems and procedures that drive the costs. This distracts the organization, constrains short-term performance, drains energy, and delays more meaningful change.

This behavior is especially evident in companies that have paid significant acquisition premiums and promised investors that the premium over the stand-alone market value will be made up by capturing cost synergies—consolidating overhead functions and support groups like customer service, utilizing excess capacity, eliminating duplicate facilities, and so on. Allowing the entire post-deal transition to be influenced by cost-reduction promises made to Wall Street is a common phenomenon in a bull market with its easy financing and inflated-stock-for-inflated-stock acquisitions. Cost reduction has become the holy grail of economic justification.

Quite simply, management needs to justify the economic wisdom of the deal—that is, the wisdom of paying unconscionable purchase premiums over market value and assuming breathtakingly high goodwill. Seemingly strategic reasons to rationalize purchase premiums always can be found. Some are more rational than others. Few are as foolproof as they seem.

Industry consolidators who outbid competitors for independent companies, for example, may have a perfectly rational market share and scale economy story to tell. Though market analysts have come to recognize that relatively few companies ever produce the higher performance level implied by the premium, they're still suckers for a good PR spin. The fact is that few companies bridge the gap between pitching the story and realizing the value.

This is even more evident for high technology. Many Wall Street market makers and even more acquirers and investors have bought the management and media hype for new, evolving technologies without challenging excessive acquisition premiums on unproven business models or nonexistent markets. The fact that new product introductions have a phenomenally high failure rate is obscured by the excitement of following a fashionable hunch. The mantra "high risk, big return" justifies a multitude of investment sins.

The current thinking is that if you expect Wall Street to bet on your roll of the dice, you must throw analysts and investors a bone. The bones thrown most often are cost synergy and scale economies. In a conference call with the analysts after announcing the deal, CEOs will deflect questions about purchase premiums by promising early and deep cost-cutting, backed by scale economies. The CFOs will reinforce the claim, soberly agreeing, and often committing to accelerated time frames for cost reduction with no more than a conceptual notion of how it will be done.

Despite public proclamations that growth is the strategic objective, early cost reductions carry the seductive lure of early returns or, at least, early recapture of premiums. They are viewed as low-hanging fruit to be picked immediately. This fruit may hang low, but it's often welded to the tree.

As the CFO shouts, "We promised the Street $100 million in savings by the third quarter," a single-minded drive to reduce cost consumes the company. An exaggerated focus on infrastructure and overhead expense builds. This usually adds up to little more than hastily planned and poorly executed downsizing, clumsy consolidation of locations, and inept disposition of surplus facilities. The main focus, though, is reduction of headcount.

> **Early cost reductions carry the seductive lure of early returns or, at least, early recapture of premiums. They are viewed as low-hanging fruit to be picked immediately. This fruit may hang low, but it's often welded to the tree.**

Little thought is given to the intricate relationship between systems, procedures, and staffing levels. Even less thought is given to which employees can or will perform in the future. All that counts is headcount. Cutting payroll takes center stage. Heads roll.

The champions of cost-cutting invariably overlook the powerful connection between staffing levels and the systems and procedures that define the work. Companies generally staff to the capability of their internal systems and practices. The company that has inefficient systems and procedures staffs more heavily than the one that has efficient systems and procedures. Eliminating staff without changing the systems they support puts a burden on the remaining employees, disrupts the work environment, and lowers productivity.

When an effort is finally made to integrate or reengineer processes and practices, choices are made on the basis of which company's *individual* practices are deemed best. These decisions are typically assigned to joint teams that are expected to set aside vested interest and make objective assessments. This practice invariably triggers a vigorous, pro-

---

Achieving Scale Economies

In the 1996 PricewaterhouseCoopers survey of mergers and acquisitions, reduction in operating expense is the fourth most frequently targeted M&A objective (by 38 percent of the respondents). However, it is the eleventh most frequently achieved (15 percent of respondents). Reducing costs invariably proves more difficult than anticipated. On the surface it appears to be a simple matter of eliminating duplication and reducing unnecessary overhead. However, the extraction of cost requires fundamentally altering work processes and procedures, redeploying people, making additional investments in training, and coping with the demoralized and overworked workforce that remains after others are laid off. Reductions in productivity of 20 to 30 percent are not uncommon, easily offsetting the paper gains that were anticipated as a result of downsizing.

longed, and acrimonious debate over which company does what better.

Downsizing can indeed yield short-term gains. If treated as a simple headcount exercise, it can result in net losses. If it is the dominant priority during the post-deal period, it will set back achievement of more meaningful economic objectives, like growth and new opportunity.

Reactive cost-cutting. Myopic restructuring. Misguided reengineering. In combination, these tactics conspire to increase cost, prolong the transition, and lower performance. There are few junctures during a major transition where the Law of Unintended Consequences manifests itself more dramatically than it does when management attempts to integrate structures, processes, and people.

Turning Camels into Racehorses

Remember the story about how a camel was created? A committee set out to design a racehorse and, committees being committees, compromised until it ended up with a camel. A lot of companies have created camels over the years. When they want to turn those camels back into racehorses, they try cutting off the humps—and they end up not with racehorses but with dead camels.

Organizations are like living creatures. They have a very intricate integrity. If they're cut too much, or cut in the wrong way, they can be destroyed.

The results of reactive cost-cutting are all the more tragic when companies find, as they often do, that they've cut too deeply and have to recruit new personnel—sometimes at a premium over past wages. The savings, always less than expected, come at the expense of the growth objectives that are at the heart of most deals.

Knee-jerk downsizing actually raises costs over the long term. Cutting staff imposes additional burdens on remaining employees, driving down productivity. Systems breakdowns, severance costs, lawsuits, early retirement programs—and, of course, losses—accumulate.

It should come as no surprise, then, that the reduction of operating expense through the capture of scale economies is one of the least achieved objectives in a merger. Over the past eight years we have conducted four surveys of mergers and acquisitions. Reducing operating ex-

The reduction of operating expense through the capture of scale economies is one of the least achieved objectives in a merger.

pense is always one of the top five objectives at the start of a transition—and one of the least frequently achieved. Reducing costs invariably proves to be more difficult to achieve than anticipated—even more so than achieving the growth-related objectives.

Why is reduction of operating cost such an elusive objective? Like most things, the problem is in the execution.

Managers saddled with aggressive and immediate headcount targets do not feel they have the time to invest in even the most rudimentary analysis. They often perceive the simple task of identifying low–value added activities that are consuming disproportionate resources as overwhelming. To most of these beleaguered lieutenants, many of whom are facing their first cataclysmic downsizing, it seems easier and faster to start heaving bodies overboard than to restructure work units. And when the only alternatives offered by consultants are rigorous and time-consuming reengineering processes that require months of data-gathering, analysis, and systems development, the old "heave-ho" doesn't sound so bad.

The quickest and most productive alternative, however, is often simply a matter of eliminating low-value added tasks. While analyzing the processes for each department of a Southern California computer manufacturer, the project manager recorded estimates of time spent on each task. On the second day of the project he noted that every department spent 5 to 10 percent of total staff time each day completing the "gold sheets"—a yellow form for recording the activities of each department. No one seemed to know how the sheets were used, who reviewed them, or whether summary reports were ever generated. Everyone resented the gold sheets but dutifully filed them at the end of each day.

Overcome with curiosity, the project manager tracked down the final repository and the guardian of the gold sheets. In a quiet corner of the accounting department sat Ellen, a pleasant, grandmotherly lady. With a sweet smile, Ellen explained everything.

> PROJECT MANAGER: *Ellen, what is it you do with these gold sheets?*
>
> ELLEN: *Each day I log them into my record book, index them, bind them, and file them in that room behind me.*
>
> PROJECT MANAGER: *And then what happens?*
>
> ELLEN: *What do you mean?*
>
> PROJECT MANAGER: *Does anyone ever look at them? Analyze them? Prepare summaries?*
>
> ELLEN: *I don't think so.*
>
> PROJECT MANAGER: *Ellen, to your knowledge, does anyone except you ever go into that file room?*
>
> ELLEN: *Never, since I started working here.*
>
> PROJECT MANAGER: *And how long has that been, Ellen?*
>
> ELLEN: *Three years. I started this job on the same day our last president left. And confidentially (whispering), I've never seen the point in all this.*

The gold sheets had been instituted by a prior president, hadn't been looked at since he left, but continued consuming resources, annoying everyone, and sapping productivity. The next day the gold sheets were eliminated. The employees cheered. The improvement in productivity—and attitude—throughout the organization was immediate and measurable.

And, no, Ellen did not lose her job. She was reassigned to something more productive and was quite a bit happier.

If management is willing to trade a little analytical accuracy for a lot of speed, there is a viable alternative to mindless downsizing (see box on Aligning Work with Priorities). It involves making quick assessments of headcount allocation and rapid redeployment decisions that make better use of people while executing a more systematic analysis of fit between systems, procedures, and number of people required. Though this alternative is less thorough than traditional business process reengineering, it does offer several advantages over simple across-the-board headcount reductions.

First, it helps to surface opportunities to redeploy people, thus pro-

Aligning Work with Priorities

Traditional reengineering often places line managers in the un-enviable position of having to defend past practices rather than creatively explore alternatives for restructuring work. The following process effectively sidesteps this disadvantage.

It focuses managers on improving the alignment between re-sources and operating priorities. It promotes constructive dialogue about redeploying staff, restructuring work, and altering work processes and procedures. It is sensible, simple, and fast, and it can be accomplished in just a few steps.

1. Identify the major end results and key activities for each work unit and then assign a relative priority to each end result based on the value drivers.
2. Estimate the time allocated to each major activity by each person in the unit. This need not be done with decimal-point accuracy. Rough estimates are sufficient.
3. Determine the cost of each end result. Major misalignments are those end results with relatively low priority and relatively high cost.
4. Simulate the financial impact of ideas for improving alignment. This helps determine which actions should be taken first.

tecting training and development investments. Second, it enables managers to simulate the financial impact of changes before those changes are made. Third, it helps identify opportunities for making deeper cuts or redeploying people based on anticipated priorities rather than on the preservation of historical practice. And fourth, it surfaces other issues that may be obstructing performance.

Cost-cutting during a transition carries greater risk and greater opportunity than at any other time. When it is anchored in even the most basic analysis of how people spend time, it presents managers with an opportunity to rapidly improve the alignment between what their people are doing and what needs to be done. Simultaneously, it helps to achieve aggressive synergy targets.

When Best Practices Become Worst Cases

Few advances in management science are potentially more lethal than design by "best practice." When combining two companies or reinventing the present company, the sum of the best practices identified rarely equals one coherent, integrated system of practices. Why? Successfully fitting one company's best practices to another company requires additional changes that go well beyond simple adoption of a new set of procedures. In addition, best practices are based on past conditions, and mergers introduce new conditions.

Generally, to make new practices work, changes must also be made in reporting relationships, measurement metrics, record-keeping, incentives, training, supervisory intensity, accountability of individuals, communications, and employee qualifications. Moreover, to be effective and not drag down performance, these changes must be made all at once, not one at a time. The high level of interdependence between structure and process prohibits an incremental approach to change.

The worst place for best practices is in mergers and acquisitions. "This is going to be a merger of equals," proclaims the CEO, hoping that these words will reassure anxious employees on both sides. Many then add, "We will take the best from both organizations." The CEO is thinking of market strengths, intellectual property, and people. To employees, however, "best practices" means everything the company does, right down to the procedure for ordering paper clips. By communicating a strategy of selecting the best from both, leaders invite open and bitter debate over everything. Managers vigorously defend past practices, and while each side attempts to convince the other of the superiority of its own procedures, the transitional organization goes into a tailspin.

These skirmishes are usually a shock to the leadership. In most mergers management expects the merged units to cooperate. But years of research in organization behavior have demonstrated that when two groups are brought together into a functional relationship, they do not cooperate. They compete. Moreover, internal competition only increases as each party attempts to gain the upper hand. Hasty attempts are made to communicate or document informal policies. People often withhold information and even produce false records. Double-counting revenues across product or service lines complicates understanding. And time is lost trying to persuade outsiders (including customers) to take a position.

Tolerating such tactics obstructs progress on key initiatives, creates distractions, and lowers morale. Failure to address these issues directly lowers productivity and contributes to divisiveness. When the matters to be resolved include core processes such as pricing, product design, purchasing, financial reporting, incentives, compensation, recruiting, performance management, and training, the negative effects can be explosive.

Why should so nonstrategic an issue as integrating operating procedures have such a devastating impact on performance? Because the processes and procedures that a company uses to get things done form a kind of organizational lymphatic system that governs the flow of information and the means for making decisions. It is unique to each business. It takes employees years to understand how it works and how to navigate through it.

When two organizations are combined, these systems can't just be grafted together, nor can people easily be plopped into a new one and expected to perform effectively. It is hard enough for individuals to adapt to unique policies and procedures when they join a new company—it creates frustration and lowers their productivity.

Of the companies surveyed in our 1996 M&A survey, 79 percent integrated operating policies and procedures subsequent to the deal. While this action was ranked fourth on a list of post-deal objectives, it ranked thirteenth in satisfaction with results. Only 54 percent of respondents reported satisfaction with integration of policies and procedures.

These results reflect the difficulty in integrating policies and procedures. The central problem here is that each company's practices reflect its own past business preferences and its unique operating style. Past successes have reinforced the wisdom of these practices in employees' minds. Thus, employees generally have a vested interest in their own past practices.

Procedural changes often require employees of an acquired company to either accept that their practices were not the best or to operate under new practices they believe may be less effective. The tendency to resist both alternatives is generally evident in internal competition, disagreement, and delayed actions.

Selectively swapping out a practice from one organization and substituting a practice from the other organization disrupts these systems in ways that are difficult to anticipate and even more difficult to correct.

Often the practices that work best together are counterintuitive. Tektronix, for example, a leader in the oscilloscope market, channels customer calls directly to the shop floor rather than filter them through a customer service department. On the surface, having shop-floor workers answer such calls would appear to be inefficient, if not bizarre. The practice does sometimes interrupt the flow of work, but it serves two very important purposes. First, it allows customers to speak with a technically qualified person who has experience with the product. Second, it allows the employees who design and manufacture the product to hear unfiltered feedback directly from the customers.

Instead of recruiting for skill sets and competencies (as is often recommended by human resource consultants), Southwest Airlines recruits for the desired attitude. Clearly this practice has implications for investments in training and development, which Southwest considers to be crucial. In addition, the CEO personally reads every employee's performance evaluation in order to stay on top of HR issues. The result is a distinctive and dominant operating style that produces a high level of customer satisfaction and loyalty.

Avoiding Deadly Combinations

In another example, a microelectronics company abandoned a set of "best practices" in favor of a set of internally aligned policies that were clearly not best practices when compared with those of their competitors.

"We have tried just about everything to improve productivity in our engineering group," said the CEO. "Better supervisors, more training, more stock options, higher salaries. Nothing seems to work. In fact, some of these changes actually have made things worse."

On the surface, this company was doing the right things. It recruited highly qualified, seasoned people, employed a disciplined screening process, paid well, linked compensation to performance, and used stock to create a sense of ownership. It applied sound performance management practices to all levels of the organization and established rigorous procedures for designing new products to help minimize mistakes.

Yet despite these "best practices," this company experienced an unacceptably high rate of new-product failure. An examination of the total system of practices revealed a clear pattern of misalignment. New-product failures were the direct result of design errors. These errors were directly attributable to mistakes made by new engineers who were unfamiliar with the design protocols and pressured to complete projects in a compressed time frame. There were many new engineers because the company had a difficult time retaining experienced engineers.

A comprehensive review of all the human resource practices further revealed that the problem was not rooted in the quality of individual policies or practices. Rather, there was something fundamentally wrong with how these practices fit together. The company hired seasoned, highly qualified engineers and then insisted that they follow detailed design procedures rather than apply their experience and discretion. The company invested in training and development, pay-for-performance, and incentive compensation, but did not promote from within. It encouraged risk-taking and entrepreneurial behavior through the use of stock options, but it also had created an environment that was intolerant of mistakes or delays.

In aggregate, the company had created several deadly combinations of practices that were increasing turnover, reducing productivity, delaying new-product introduction, lowering the revenue growth rate, and decreasing shareholder value. The obvious solution was to eliminate misalignments—to optimize the total system of practices by suboptimizing some of the parts, not engaging in a search for new programs to retain key engineering staff.

Though counterintuitive, the tactics made complete sense when viewed from the perspective of the total system. Reduce the use of stock options. Shift the recruiting strategy toward more college hires. Invest more in training and development at the entry levels. Decrease variable pay. These practices were clearly not the best practices, yet they made far better sense in conjunction with a product design strategy that placed a premium on procedural compliance, scrupulous attention to detail, and a willingness to adopt the company's way of designing products.

Hull Speed—It's the System, Stupid!

Boat designers always wrestle with something called hull speed. A boat can go only as fast as the hull design allows. Once maximum hull speed is reached, the craft cannot be made to go faster, even with larger engines or more sail. To go faster, the hull must be redesigned. But hull redesign can have a profound impact on safety, stability, handling, and cargo space. All of these factors must be considered simultaneously when designing a boat.

The same principle applies to the design (or redesign) of an organization's systems, procedures, and structure. Decisions about processes and structure have profound productivity implications that extend well beyond the layers and headcounts. Existing work groups are altered or disbanded; new work groups are created; work and decision flows are changed; individual roles and accountabilities are revamped; the superior/subordinate status of individuals is modified. Behavior, motivation, and, ultimately, the capture of shareholder value are affected.

Creating a coherent set of processes during a major transition, as one CEO remarked, is tantamount to "trying to improve police procedures during a gun battle."

Organizations enter a merger or acquisition as fully functioning, self-contained *systems* of processes and practices. Selectively swapping out a practice from one organization and substituting a practice from the other organization disrupts these systems in ways that are difficult to anticipate and even more difficult to correct. Tinkering simply doesn't work. It can initiate a chain reaction of miscues and disruptions that eventually snowball into large-scale breakdowns.

Tinkering with a Railroad

The 1996 combination of Union Pacific and Southern Pacific was supposed to save $800 million a year. But in the first full year following the merger UP reduced earnings by 35 percent and slashed its dividend in half. Facing a roomful of furious customers, Union Pacific's chairman, Dick Davidson, confessed that problems with Southern Pacific were proving "much harder to fix than I ever imagined."

Historically, Union Pacific had been the more successful railroad. It had better managers, track, regional yards, locomotives, and computers. It operated on a much larger scale than SP and wasted little time or money on inefficient routes.

By comparison, Southern Pacific was a beleaguered money-loser with few profitable trains and aging equipment. The important Houston switching yard contained too few locomotives, outdated computers, and sagging, misaligned track that was too short to handle most trains.

On paper, the deal should have worked—Southern Pacific had much to gain from its merger with Union Pacific.

"Blame for why the merger went so badly has been laid on everything but plague and swarming locusts: Computer problems. Bizarre labor rules. Inept federal regulators. Weather. Mexico. An intimidating CEO with subordinates reluctant to deliver bad news. Surging grain traffic. A booming petrochemical industry. But mostly the problem was arrogance. Union Pacific refused to accept suggestions from Southern Pacific employees who knew how to run their ailing railroad with chewing gum and baling wire. When UP tried to impose its way of doing things on the very fragile Southern Pacific, service went haywire" (*Fortune*, March 30, 1998).

Consider the following example. Two medium-sized technology companies have decided to merge. The larger company has been in business for over four decades, the smaller company for just under ten years. The larger company experiences about 3 percent turnover of its professional staff and has an average length of service of fourteen years. Seventy-five percent of all its non-entry-level job openings are filled from within. The smaller company suffers from 20 percent turnover and has an average length of service of four years. Only 30 percent of its non-entry-level job openings are filled from within. Both companies offer generous stock option and stock purchase plans that cover most of the professional staff.

In spite of public proclamations about "compatibility," these two companies have distinctive operating styles and distinctive policies and procedures that support their respective cultures. The larger company has spent four decades building what economists call *firm-specific* human capital (a workforce of people with knowledge, skills, and abilities that are most useful within their own company). Its policies and procedures are aligned with its culture. This company brings people in at lower levels, moves them up through the organization, and then filters them out over time. It has many economic advantages, but continuing innovation is not one of them.

The smaller company, on the other hand, is a revolving door for employees. It has higher training costs, lower profitability, and more wrongful-discharge lawsuits. It bleeds human capital at the rate of 20 percent per year, but it also introduces three times as many new products as its larger counterpart. And since the major reason for the deal is growth, preserving the capability to introduce new products rapidly is one of the top value drivers.

Now consider the challenge facing managers as they attempt to integrate just the human resource policies of these two companies. If they line up the practices from each company and begin adopting those they deem the best, they run the very real risk of building their own version of a policy camel— an "all-star" collection of human resource management processes

> **The kind of reengineering that must be done in the middle of a major transition is like operating a MASH unit. It's not pretty. It's not perfect. But it saves lives.**

that has no hope of helping managers actually manage human resources.

The System Is the Solution

The task facing managers who must integrate core processes and procedures in the wake of a merger is a similar challenge. While there is no simple way to integrate myriad practices, the following steps have proved useful to many who have attempted to slog their way through the procedural bog created by a merger or acquisition.

1: *Defer to the value drivers.* For the time being, push aside any policy or procedure that does not have a direct impact on, or provide critical support to, a value-driving action. There is not enough time during a transition to reconfigure policies and procedures that were developed over decades. Time spent shuffling the infrastructure is not an acceptable excuse for poor service, missed shipments, or delays in introducing new products. This is the time for ruthless prioritization.

2: *Identify critical interdependencies.* The policies and practices most likely to surface as high priorities will relate to sales, operations, and development or to the selection, training, and motivation of people. The transition teams responsible for integrating these practices must be required to identify critical interdependencies and potentially deadly combinations before any consolidation begins.

3: *Reengineer in a compressed time frame.* Small room. No windows. Plenty of caffeine and candy. Don't come out until it's done. There is plenty of brainpower already available to make reasonable decisions and to brainstorm good ideas.

The purpose is not to create model processes for future generations but to ensure that the policies or procedures in question adequately support the value drivers. No more white papers. No further study. No more benchmarking. No more sending it back to committee.

The kind of reengineering that must be done in the middle of a major transition is like operating a MASH unit. It's not pretty. It's not perfect. But it saves lives.

∎∎∎

Mergers, acquisitions, and large-scale changes present companies with an unprecedented opportunity to make sweeping changes, leave legacy practices behind, and ensure that people are redeployed to work on activities that add real value. Since investors, employees, the community, and other stakeholders anticipate major changes during a transition, companies that act quickly and decisively can shield themselves from the negative public relations and financial discounting that tends to accompany protracted restructuring.

Companies that prefer to move at a more leisurely pace or that allow themselves to be distracted by low-value-added initiatives, end up testing the outer limits of stakeholder patience. When these companies finally get around to reorganizing, restructuring, and redeploying, they discover that their actions are now being inspected under much harsher light.

11

The Ultimate Scapegoat

Unconventional Advice About Culture

The first time we saw Buzz Thurman, he was grinning maniacally at us, and a million other Americans, from the cover of Business Week under a headline touting him as "America's New Gen-X Tycoon." He was the twenty-five-year-old whiz-kid founder of Starlink, a small technology start-up with a piece of software that promised to revolutionize communications.

Born in Colorado, the brainy son of Boulder's best television repairman, Buzz had flabbergasted his teachers by skipping two years of high school, whizzing through UC-Berkeley on a full scholarship, and, at the age of nineteen, earning a doctorate in computer science. A few years later, messing around in his father's junk-filled garage, Buzz came up with the prototype for Starlink, an impressive enabling technology for compression and encryption of direct satellite broadcasts. It held the promise of a totally secure "Internet via satellite," without the bandwidth limitations of current technology.

Anyone with a television set could access any person, any business, any data, anywhere in the world, at a ridiculously low cost. No waiting, no hacking, no worries about security, no need for a computer or expensive software. Buzz had invented the communications equivalent of the cure for cancer.

With two equally brainy buddies, Buzz formed Starlink—the company—to work out the remaining bugs and bring a salable product to market. All the fledgling needed was more capital to finish development, some marketing muscle, and a distribution channel. Venture capitalists wanted an unbearable 85 percent of the business for their investment. The second option was to license an application of Starlink's compression algorithm to the coven of networking companies and corporate intranet czars searching for a bandwidth solution. It would give Starlink a customer base, a beachhead, and cash—but not enough cash.

Enter Will Doors, the nation's uncrowned electronic emperor and techie superhero. Ready to make Buzz Thurman and his brainy buddies rich beyond their wildest dreams, Doors and his mighty Macropolis gladly offered a mere $3 billion for the burgeoning Starlink Company and all the rights to its intellectual property. Talk of the merger filled the airwaves. Even Larry King interviewed Doors and Thurman in one of the most impenetrable encounters between celebrity babble and computerspeak ever recorded.

Knee-knocking fear gripped computer and communications companies everywhere—for them, Starlink was Armageddon. The frenzy triggered throughout those industries by the Starlink-Macropolis deal was matched only by the near panic it sparked on Wall Street, where technology stocks had long leveraged the S&P 500, shaped the fate of mutual funds, and become the oxygen enabling Dow climbers to conquer one market peak after another.

People magazine, taking over where Business Week left off, chronicled the life and lifestyle of Buzz Thurman. Still the loving son he'd always been, Buzz spent some of his newfound billions to build his father a new Boulder garage—a high-rise looming fifteen stories out of the family's backyard—and People's photographers captured it for all the world to envy. Nobody missed the old garage. Why should they? Disney had paid $2 million for it and shipped it to Orlando for an EPCOT tribute to "America's Garage Geniuses"—those humble tinkerers, ranging from Thomas Edison to Dave Packard to Buzz Thurman, who have wired this country in more ways than one.

The reason you've never heard of Buzz—and who keeps old copies of Business Week?—*is that his fifteen minutes of fame occurred several years ago, an eternity on the celebrity screen. And for all intents and purposes, the Boulder wunderkind became history before the ink was dry on his Macropolis merger contract. To be sure, Thurman entered the partnership with high hopes and the best of intentions, just as most marriage partners do. But the postnuptial bliss evaporated quickly when it became apparent that Starlink had been submerged, not merged.*

What really happened when Will Doors bought Starlink—lock, stock, and CPU?

In a nutshell, Macropolis mobilized its huge PR department, commandeered bandwidth throughout the Internet, and trumpeted the merger across the planet. What it overlooked in its communications orgy, however, were the people who had the most to gain—or lose—in the deal: the Starlink employees, current customers who could be converted, and Macropolis' own shareholders and alliance partners in other communications ventures.

Macropolis knew, of course, that it needed to hang on to Buzz's design engineers to get a fully operational Starlink device on the market in a timely fashion. So it dropped a few million in signing bonuses and generous stock options in the parent company. A few hints were dropped about a phantom royalty plan based on the device's revenue.

As for the fattest cat, Doors himself spoke only once to any Starlink employees, choosing the occasion of the young company's first and last annual softball game to orate on the Macropolis future and hand out Macropolis baseball caps to Starlink's bewildered staff.

As soon as the deal closed, Starlink management found itself trapped in endless meetings about the organization's structure, Macropolis design reviews, compatibility with Macropolis products, consistency with the Macropolis GUI, benefit plans, and consolidation of facilities. Buzz's top software engineer broke out in hives because he hadn't set foot in the lab for six weeks. With no one talking to the design staff, it didn't take long for the rumor mill to begin churning out several juicy scenarios.

About this time, the Macropolis VP of engineering decided to do design reviews at each stage of final development of the Starlink device. Buzz's crew was fit to be tied. They knew this guy didn't have the tech-

nical expertise, not to mention the fact that he was a pompous boor. Used to the laid-back, entrepreneurial style at Starlink, they had pegged the VP right from the start as someone for whom process took precedence over outcome.

Two engineers jumped ship after they heard rumors that (1) Buzz was dead, (2) the merger was in trouble, and (3) Macropolis engineering was going to bring in a crack team to finish the product without them. The last rumor seemed particularly plausible since the team had made no serious progress on the device for over two months. How could they? All the internal issues, including the mechanics of becoming employees of the monolithic Macropolis, were major distractions.

When a Macropolis board member read a newspaper article a few months later about a new communication technology involving lasers, he fired off a nasty note to Will Doors: "This story says the laser technology will revolutionize the computer and communications industry. I thought we were going to revolutionize the industry! Why the hell did we pay that huge premium for Starlink anyway?"

Within a year all of Starlink's best and brightest had either departed or succumbed to inertia. The vision had languished, opportunity had been lost, focus was obscured, and progress had stalled. And where was Buzz Thurman? At Disney World, shaking hands and reading a flakhoned speech at the ceremony opening Dad's garage to hordes of vacationers rolling about in strollers and wheelchairs.

Within eighteen months competitors had begun to catch up and Starlink's competitive advantage was deteriorating faster than last year's Macropolis product line. Will Doors, in a conference call with Wall Street analysts and institutional investors, shrugged it off as a classic case of irreconcilable conflict between two companies' cultures.

In truth, it was a classic case of a botched transition, but everyone nodded sagely on hearing the culture alibi.

Culture—The Ultimate Scapegoat

Corporate culture—the set of entrenched behaviors that characterize how a company gets things done—has become the ultimate scapegoat and preferred whipping boy of failed mergers and acquisitions. When a deal is announced, analysts publicly worry about cultural compatibility between the two companies. Senior executives wonder about whether the company cultures will fit together. And when the new company fails to meet financial projections, the executives say, "The fundamentals were good. We just couldn't get past the culture clash."

Cultural incompatibility has been blamed for disrupting even the most promising business opportunities. The history of corporate marriages is replete with tales of cultural mismatch, endless squabbling, and outright disaster.

In 1984 IBM and Rolm apparently became instant victims of cultural incompatibility. IBM's staid corporate culture clashed spectacularly with that of the more relaxed Santa Clara telecommunications company. After five years of disappointment IBM admitted defeat. It sold Rolm to Siemens AG for less than half what it had paid.

Consider the case of Hewlett-Packard and Apollo Computers. With no knowledge of how to integrate the two organizational structures, or of the Apollo culture, the H-P acquisition team handed integration planning and decision making to line management as soon as the deal was completed. When several key Apollo executives subsequently departed, an H-P general manager was appointed to run the Apollo division. The cultural divide was succinctly illustrated by the characterization of H-P people as the Stepford Wives and Apollo people as the Hell's Angels.

The litany of star-crossed marriages spans all industry sectors and includes such notables as AT&T and NCR, Sperry & Burroughs, Bridgestone and Firestone, Synoptics Communications and Wellfleet Communications, Republic and Northwest Airlines, Wells Fargo and First Interstate, USAir and PSA, Sony and Columbia-TriStar, Bank of America and Charles Schwab, Novell and WordPerfect, GTE and Contel, Sybase and Powersoft, Acer and Altos Computers, Union Pacific and Southern Pacific, and others.

The cultural divide was succinctly illustrated by the characterization of H-P people as the Stepford Wives and Apollo people as the Hell's Angels.

In the 1996 PricewaterhouseCoopers survey on mergers and acquisitions, 49 percent of the respondents reported differences in operating philosophy as the most troublesome post-deal difficulty. Moreover, cultural differences were perceived to have incurred substantial cost in terms of lost business opportunity. That same year, in a change management survey conducted by PricewaterhouseCoopers and the *Wall Street Journal* (Europe), 54 percent of the respondents reported that culture was the main obstacle they encountered in implementing change. Invariably, culture appears at the top of everyone's problem list, whether the objective is to merge, acquire, or initiate major change.

As these findings show, culture is widely vilified as the biggest killer of deals and the greatest obstacle to change. It is blamed for delaying progress, distracting management, destroying morale, and dissolving shareholder value. Convenient though it may be, this blame is misplaced. Though cultural differences are undeniably a challenge, culture is rarely the culprit.

Many accusers claim that corporate culture is like a career criminal, an incorrigible hard luck case beyond rehabilitation. They may insist that a company's culture cannot be changed quickly, doesn't mix well with other cultures, and is indifferent to passionate sermons about vision and values. But, more to the point, it's easier for an executive to place blame on such a plausible suspect than to shoulder responsibility for destroying billions of dollars in shareholder value.

Over the years armies of change management consultants have brainwashed executives into believing that culture is a nearly intractable force that takes time, patience, and persistence to alter. Start, they say, by articulating a common vision. Agree on shared values. Craft the communications. Laminate the results and plaster posters everywhere. Conduct half-day workshops with middle management. Then wait. Eventually everybody will believe and behave differently.

Not a chance.

The corporate victims of this scam are still waiting.

Four Myths of Culture Change and Integration

Four common myths about culture change have emerged in the popular literature and now enjoy widespread acceptance.

Myth 1—*Cultural Incompatibility Is the Biggest Cause of Post-deal Failure*

Don't believe it. Quaker Oats lost $500 million of market value with the announcement of the Snapple acquisition, long before anyone attempted integration. Dow Jones' disappointments with Telerate and Eli Lilly's setback with PCS Health Services had more to do with questionable strategy, overpayment, and weak execution than cultural mismatch.

Cultural differences in operating style, customer relations, and communications represent formidable obstacles to post-merger integration. But it is a huge leap to claim that these differences are the torpedoes that sink the company. Independent analyses more typically cite other factors as the cause of failure—poor strategic fit, overpayment, inept execution, slow decision making, failure to achieve timely integration of core information systems, and clumsy, or nonexistent, due diligence at the beginning. Our own studies suggest that the culprit is lack of focus on value-driving actions and delays in generating early momentum toward the capture of shareholder value.

> **Cultural differences in operating style, customer relations, and communications represent formidable obstacles to post-merger integration. But it is a huge leap to claim that these differences are the torpedoes that sink the company.**

Perhaps cultural incompatibility carries most of the blame for post-deal failure because every company has unspoken prejudices about the merger partner. These prejudices include perceptions formed in direct competition or as a result of biases about the merger partner's industry or market segment, technology, management or even distribution channel. The bias may be positive or negative, but it's bias nonetheless.

Initially most companies avoid friction by diplomatically sidestep-

> **Diplomatic sidestepping of differences simply postpones resolution at a time when speed is essential. It produces a slow, awkward compromise that frustrates the most talented and achievement-oriented people. It can lead to conflict, an exodus of top talent, and economic extinction.**

ping differences in opinion and approach. But as Winston Churchill once noted, "Diplomacy is the art of saying, 'Nice doggy,' while looking for a rock." Though it may appear to be a safer path, it is not.

Diplomatic sidestepping of differences simply postpones resolution at a time when speed is essential. It produces a slow, awkward compromise that frustrates the most talented and achievement-oriented people. It can lead to conflict, an exodus of top talent, and economic extinction.

Innovation is the cornerstone of corporate opportunity. Intellectual and cultural inbreeding present the greatest obstacles to innovation. Companies that grow by acquiring other companies that are culturally distinct are taking bold steps to refresh their intellectual gene pool. Though it is never easy and frequently painful, such an acquisition offers options for growth and strengthens competitive position.

Far from being a major cause of failure, differences in culture can stimulate new vitality if they are not smothered. They can be a source of competitive strength and business differentiation.

Myth 2—Culture Is an Intractable Force

Despite clear evidence of differences in operating tactics, management philosophy, communication style, policies, and practices, most CEOs, upon announcing a deal, make bold statements about the compatibility of the two company cultures. Questions about differences are dismissed with humorous reference to idiosyncratic appearance, dress, or mannerisms.

No CEO announces a deal with the disclaimer: "If we can just reconcile the differences between how our two companies operate. . . ." However, when very real differences in culture manifest themselves in confusion over marketing strategy, selling tactics, customer service approaches, product design processes, communication practices, and so on, the glib comments about cultural peculiarities migrate to harsh statements about entrenched behavior and antiquated business practices. Culture quickly becomes the intractable force that is denying

When very real differences in culture manifest themselves in confusion over marketing strategy, selling tactics, customer service approaches, product design processes, communication practices, and so on, the glib comments about cultural peculiarities migrate to harsh statements about entrenched behavior and antiquated business practices.

shareholders the cost synergies and growth opportunities promised by the dealmakers.

Culture, though, is one of the more manageable variables, if it is understood. The problems that managers experience lie not with culture per se, but with their inability to perceive the culture well enough to understand how it functions in their own organization (or one they might acquire) and how they might manage it to drive economic value. This understanding begins with accepting culture as a set of characteristic behaviors rather than a collection of espoused values or beliefs. Thus understood, culture is manageable, if not malleable.

Myth 3—Cultures Can Be Blended Gradually

Despite overwhelming evidence of the need to address cultural differences swiftly, many executives persist in believing that it is possible to merge the cultures of two companies gradually, through contact and interaction. Ironically, social scientists of the 1950s used to refer to this discredited strategy as the "contagion approach." The attitude of these optimistic executives can be summed up as follows: "We will create a merger of equals. We'll take our culture and add their culture. We will get a blended culture. The best of both will emerge."

Fat chance.

No Such Thing as a Merger of Equals

In the Galápagos Islands, there lives a species of waterfowl called a booby. Some boobies have red feet, and some have blue feet.

Once upon a time a group of inquisitive naturalists wondered what would happen if a red-footed booby mated with a blue-footed booby. Would the baby boobies have one red foot and one blue foot? Or, more exciting still, would purple-footed boobies emerge? Or some other color?

Eager to test their hypothesis, the naturalists rounded up a few pairs of cooperative boobies and encouraged them to mate.

When the boobies began to hatch, there was some disappointment among the matchmakers. As one after another baby booby emerged from its egg, it had either two red feet or two blue feet. There was not a purple, or even a mauve, foot in the bunch.

It was Mother Nature's way of saying there is no such thing as a merger of equals.

Business cultures also tend to be either red or blue. Yet many executives in the midst of mergers and acquisitions confuse cultural harmony with cultural homogeneity. Believing they can successfully blend the best of two organizations, they attempt to create a purple-footed corporate booby.

Were this Mix-Master mentality only misguided, it could be dismissed as harmless folly. Unfortunately, it is also dangerous because it delays the transition and actually slows cultural integration and the creation of shareholder value.

Myth 4—Culture Can Be Changed by Preaching Vision and Values

Another dangerous group is the executive team that believes it can merge cultures simply by communicating a common set of values. "Start with a set of shared values," some experts intone, "and build a new culture around those shared values." This thought process is breathtakingly deluded. Why? Consider the following scenario.

They hammer out a set of common values (universal platitudes) that only Charles Manson could disagree with and an idealistic vision of corporate opportunity that only Karl Marx would dispute.

The senior executives of two recently merged companies go on an off-site retreat. In pastoral surroundings, and under the guidance of a facilitator, they serendipitously discover they have similar beliefs. Thereupon, they hammer out a set of common values (universal platitudes) that only Charles Manson could disagree with and an idealistic vision of corporate opportunity that only Karl Marx would dispute.

This shared vision and set of common values finds its way into memos, employee newsletters, and shareholder reports and is displayed on company posters. Like the singing of the national anthem before all sporting events, these words become part of every speech, public pronouncement, and press release.

Q: Will the employees agree with these statements of vision and values?

A: Probably.

Q: If asked, will the employees be able to say they have observed management behavior consistent with these utopian values in the past? Or that they have observed management behavior consistent with these utopian values in the current interaction between the two firms?

A: Not likely, and not likely.

Q: Will the statement of shared values influence the characteristic behavior of each executive who contributed to the statements of vision and values?

A: *Not likely.*

Q: *Will individual executives and employees continue to behave as they did in the past?*

A: *Yes.*

Q: *Will the statement of common values change the behavior of individual employees?*

A: *Not unless management changes its behavior first. And certainly not without an infrastructure that recognizes and rewards behavior change.*

Q: *Will the act of articulating common values bridge cultural incompatibilities and lead to new behaviors?*

A: *No. People do not necessarily behave in ways that are consistent with the beliefs and attitudes they claim to hold.*
For example: "We hold these truths to be self-evident. That all men are created equal. . . . " Thus begins the Declaration of Independence. The gentlemen who signed that document cononed, or at least accepted, the widespread practice of slavery. They articulated an ideal but continued to behave in ways that were more personally rewarding—socially, politically, and financially.

Q: *Can you justifiably expect employees who are living with uncertainty after their lives have been disrupted by merger or gut-wrenching change to exhibit more compliance with new company values than did the signers of the Declaration of Independence?*

A: *No.*

Culture can't be blended like a milkshake, nor can it be changed by passionate sermons, newsletters, screen savers, or success posters. It's not about hype, promotion, mantras, or prayers. Cultural integration is about behavior change—not rhetoric.

Herein lies a fundamental problem with trying to change culture by preaching vision, values, truths, or beliefs. It just doesn't work.

Bless you, Lou Gerstner, for turning IBM around without stopping to draft a statement of vision and values.

Culture can't be blended like a milkshake, nor can it be changed by passionate sermons, newsletters, screen savers, or success posters. It's not about hype, promotion, mantras, or prayers. Cultural integration is about behavior change—not rhetoric.

Statements of vision and shared values are only a starting point. The real engine of culture change is the observable behavior of highly visible executives and key manager role models. Bless you, Lou Gerstner, for turning IBM around without stopping to draft a statement of vision and values.

Culture Is Not the Culprit

Collectively, the four myths of culture change and integration reinforce a widely held belief that culture is a major cause of failure in mergers and acquisitions. The problem, however, has not been culture. The failure lies in management's standard solution. Time, cohabitation, and aggressive communication of core values will not alter behavior or integrate culture. This is the wrong solution.

Integrating two cultures requires focusing on the idiosyncratic behavior of the two companies, not the values they claim to hold. You can no more drive cultural integration by communicating shared values than an advertiser can persuade you to change your buying habits simply by increasing ad space. Like the advertiser, you need to provide more powerful inducements.

Culture becomes a very convenient alibi when post-deal profits plummet. If you want to continue using this alibi with a clear conscience, skip the rest of this chapter.

Changing Culture Means Changing Behavior

Imagine that each morning every person woke up and thought, "Okay, how do I need to behave today? Let's see, sales staff meeting at

> **One of the more humorous (if not prophetic) definitions of insanity is "doing the same thing over and over again and expecting different results." To a large extent many people are guilty of a form of behavioral insanity. They enter different situations all the time but rely on the same behaviors that have produced results for them in the past.**

9:00 A.M., performance review for one of my sales reps at 11:00. New-product meeting in the afternoon. Well, looks as if I'm going to need to use a lot of self-control and flexibility in the morning. In the afternoon, I'll need to shift gears a bit and be creative and persuasive."

Where would we find such a scenario? Most likely in an episode out of *The Twilight Zone*.

Although there is nothing that prevents people from planning to adapt, the fact is that people don't. People put on coats when it's cold and wear short sleeves when it's hot, but they confront every work-related situation wearing the same old tattered behavioral "clothing."

One of the more humorous (if not prophetic) definitions of insanity is "doing the same thing over and over again and expecting different results." To a large extent many people are guilty of a form of behavioral insanity. They enter different situations all the time but rely on the same behaviors that have produced results for them in the past. Do they assess each situation and think: What am I trying to accomplish? Why is that difficult? Which behaviors in my repertoire are most appropriate?

Not a chance. They act out of habit.

What's worse is that each person will argue vehemently that he or she is flexible and can adapt to new situations. There is no question that people have the *ability* to adapt behavior, but few do it very often. They need the proper inducements—role models, recognition, rewards (both tangible and psychic), and peer support.

Companies exhibit the same tendency to approach new challenges with the entrenched behaviors that make up their culture. Unfortunately, when companies merge or embark on a major change, when value drivers change, and when success depends on new behaviors, the current culture—past practices and habits—often ceases to be the most effective way of conducting business. Instead, it becomes an insurmountable obstacle to progress.

Organizational culture change or integration must start with behavior at the individual level.

Let's start with one person. Consider the case of the free-throwing paperboy.

We knew an eminent CEO who loved to get up early in his Lake Forest manse and peacefully peruse the Wall Street Journal *over his morning coffee. Rain or shine, he would stride out to the long driveway in his Armani bathrobe, peer around, and promptly throw a fit. The* Journal *always arrived—he would hear the paperboy's bike tires crunching on the driveway gravel—but it never arrived in the same place. Our indignant and rather overweight friend, panting and soaked with dew, found the paper behind the hedge, in the rosebushes, on the terrace far from his front door. Why couldn't that idiot kid aim it at the designated spot, his top front step?*

The CEO had no time or patience for this early-morning paper chase, this daily violation of his important space. He tried everything to stop it. He called the kid's boss, he called the kid's mother, he hid behind a huge oak tree and jumped out to browbeat the wretch when he showed up.

"Leave my Journal *here, damn it!" the CEO cried. "Here!"*

Nothing worked.

The paperboy had his own rules. He had lots of homework and a very long paper route. He had to get through it fast. To him, it didn't make a dime's worth of difference where the Journal *landed. Once it left his hands, he was gone, burning rubber to the next customer. He firmly believed he was right—or not wrong anyway.*

This impasse went on for weeks. The CEO nearly canceled his subscription. The paperboy treated him like the blowhard he was rapidly becoming. His glamorous wife called him "bore-ing"—the paper caper wasn't her only provocation—and before long she slipped off to Venice for an experimental reunion with one of her two former husbands.

That did it. The CEO finally had to stop abusing his brain and start using it. Once he cooled down, the solution popped into his head.

The next day the paperboy zipped up the driveway as usual, cocked his arm for the toss, and stopped short. Bolted to the front door was a beautiful new basketball net. The boy stared at the net, smiled, and took aim. The Journal *soared through the net and thunked to the ground, precisely where the CEO wanted it delivered.*

From then on the boy netted the Journal *every morning, week after week, and the happy CEO got his daily financial fix, from puts to pork bellies.*

You're probably wondering two things: Is there a point to this story? And whatever happened to his wife?

Yes, and don't know.

The point is, you can't get people to change their attitudes and beliefs just by talk, sweet or sour, or even by threats.

Behavior, though, is something else. Beliefs are stubborn. Behavior is flexible. It's easier to get people to try new behaviors than to alter their beliefs. If you can get them to try new behaviors, and if you can reinforce those behaviors with some personal reward or inducement, they will repeat the behavior. With multiple repetitions, beliefs gradually shift to align with the rewarded behaviors. This is the beginning of behavior change, and it is a prerequisite to changing culture.

It is easier to transform corporate culture following a merger or acquisition than at any other time. Investors, customers, suppliers, and employees all expect changes to occur. The marketplace is primed. The workforce is ready. Management is eager to get under way. However, many companies fail to recognize, let alone take advantage of, the window of opportunity. And whether or not the company realizes it, once the new management team is selected and announced, the cultural concrete has already started to set.

Overcoming cultural incompatibility doesn't require heavy equipment. The CEO changed the paperboy's behavior as soon as he could provide both a clear objective and an immediate reward. Defining desired behaviors, deploying role models, providing meaningful incentives, and avoiding muddled messages are the only culture change tools a company needs.

Defining the Moments

In the movie *Tin Cup*, a happy-go-lucky, underachieving golf pro named Roy McAvoy finds himself miraculously playing in the U.S. Open. Tied for the lead on the final day of the tournament, he faces a critical decision on a very difficult shot on the last hole: take a big risk, go for the green, and win, or play it safe, make par, and force a playoff. Risk it all or play it safe?

This is a defining event for Roy. In his own inimitable fashion, and using his favorite expression, Roy sums up the situation: "Define the moment, or the moment defines you." Roy's life has been marked by a tangled skein of "defining moments," and he always takes the risk. This time is no exception. He goes for the green.

> **Corporate cultures are defined by how employees characteristically handle pivotal business situations that present an opportunity to perform in an extraordinary and distinctive manner. The behaviors of managers and employees under these circumstances determine the company's culture.**

Every day employees in every company face defining moments. Sometimes these moments involve taking a risk or playing it safe. They usually revolve around an unsupervised choice about how best to perform an important business function. This is when the organization's true culture kicks in.

Corporate cultures are defined by how employees characteristically handle pivotal business situations that present an opportunity to perform in an extraordinary and distinctive manner. The behaviors of managers and employees under these circumstances determine the company's culture. These are the situations that regularly test whether the company walks the talk or just talks the talk.

Suppose, for example, that a patient gets angry because she cannot get a follow-up appointment to see her regular physician as soon as she would like. How does the scheduling clerk handle the angry patient? Or what if a customer's car breaks down shortly after the warranty expires. Do the service representatives follow the rules, make an exception, or pursue another alternative? Perhaps a design engineer discovers incomplete documentation on manufacturing specifications and decides to

By consistently reinforcing—through role models and rewards—the correct choices, a company shapes its culture. Consistent reinforcement leads to a kind of "behavioral memory" that takes over and drives desired behaviors in times of crisis.

hold up the production release. How does she handle the various individuals, including the CEO, who will be more than a little upset about the delay?

Dilemmas like these present defining moments for the people in an organization. The choices they make not only influence customer satisfaction, productivity, and profitability but also establish a standard of behavior. By consistently reinforcing—through role models and rewards—the correct choices, a company shapes its culture. Consistent reinforcement leads to a kind of "behavioral memory" that takes over and drives desired behaviors in times of crisis.

In 1994 Intel faced a defining event. A logic flaw in the Pentium processor was discovered long after millions had been shipped, installed, and put in use by customers. A superior technology company and innovative leader, Intel had built its culture around original equipment manufacturers, not the end user. Because the flaw was insignificant for most applications, and because the cost of recall and replacement was prohibitive, Intel decided to replace the processor for those who insisted and to downplay the flaw for the rest. What it didn't anticipate was consumer reaction.

Rumors flew on the Internet. The stock price tumbled. Competitors attacked Intel's integrity. Bowed but unbroken, Intel relented, replaced the part, and invested millions of dollars to polish its tarnished market image.

This defining event put the company's collective behavior to the test. If

Statements about strategic and economic benefits must be converted into straightforward behavioral examples of how people will be expected to operate in the post-deal environment.

Intel had had a long history of experience in dealing with end users, it probably would have behaved differently. But it hadn't, and it didn't. In the end the loss of market image far outweighed the cost of replacing the equipment.

The other side of the coin was exhibited by Saturn's reaction some years back upon learning that it had shipped new cars with defective coolant. Rather than taking the traditional route of mailing out recall notices and sending radiator-replacement kits to dealers, Saturn recalled all the cars and ground them up. That's right, it turned them into landfill. For a "new kind of car company," its reputation for quality and responsible manufacturing was far more important than the cost of making scrap metal the expensive way.

The task of fine-tuning a company's culture following a merger or acquisition should not be delegated to staff departments like human resources. The responsibility for identifying the defining events and articulating desired behaviors rests in the hands of operating managers who direct delivery of products and services to customers.

Defining desired behaviors should begin with the value driver analysis. It is not enough to begin pontificating about compatibility or to generalize about cultural characteristics. Statements about strategic and economic benefits must be converted into straightforward behavioral examples of how people will be expected to operate in the post-deal environment.

For example, with newly configured sales territories, how will sales representatives be expected to influence customers in order to smoothly transfer long-term relationships? How will employees who have direct customer contact be expected to interact with each other in order to sell a broader value proposition to customers? How will service managers be expected to motivate their staff to maintain high levels of service and rapid response times while simultaneously meeting aggressive cost-reduction targets?

The Role of Cultural Role Models

Q: If corporate culture is the sum of the idiosyncratic behaviors a company's employees characteristically use to perform their jobs, how do employees learn the behaviors?

A: *Children learn to deal with the world around them by watching and copying the characteristic behaviors and communication styles of their parents, their friends, and other role models whom they regard highly for their social, athletic, academic, or other successes. Likewise, employees learn to function in companies by watching and emulating the characteristic behavior and using the language of co-workers and highly visible managers who have achieved status, recognition, and rewards within the company. This is how culturally consistent behaviors are learned and passed on to others.*

Q: *How does a characteristic set of behaviors become entrenched in the organization?*

A: *Co-workers and managers who have achieved status through formal recognition and reward (monetary and nonmonetary) are role models. At the very least, other employees identify with these role models and tend to adopt their behavior or experiment with it. Even when employees fail to identify with the role models, the consistently employed and readily observed behaviors and language of these individuals tend to be emulated precisely because other employees and managers want to enjoy similar recognition and reward.*

This is how certain behaviors become entrenched in a culture. It is no accident that Nordstrom, which actively rewards, recognizes, and promotes heroic deeds, has employees dedicated to providing heroic service. That is what is expected, that is where the recognition is, and that is where the rewards are.

Q: *How long should culture change or integration take?*

A: *Contrary to popular belief, culture change can be accomplished in a relatively brief period of time—a matter of months. The company must be willing to fill its most visible positions with people who exemplify the new "ideal" culture, and it must publicly recognize those who actively engage in the desired behaviors.*

The implications for culture change and integration should be clear. If you want to shape a new culture or adopt behaviors consistent with the company's values, select role models who exemplify the desired behaviors and deploy them in visible positions of authority throughout the company. Be generous and public with your recognition of their performance.

This sends a signal to the rest of the employees. You will be making it clear that the path to success in your company is in emulating these behaviors. In doing this, you will be "walking the talk" and reinforcing the desired culture.

Selecting and Deploying Role Models

Selecting, deploying, and publicly recognizing role models is a fundamental step in securing culture change. Companies that fail to take this step will fail in their efforts to change or integrate cultures. These failures are common for several reasons:

Reason 1

Many executives think they know what they are looking for when selecting role models for key positions. But in fact, if the company has not identified defining moments and methodically described corresponding behaviors, it does not have the necessary guidelines to select role models whose behavior is aligned with the value drivers. Moreover, the behavior of the selected role models will not be consistent. The lack of consistency creates internal confusion over precisely which behaviors are valued.

> **If you want to shape a new culture or adopt behaviors consistent with the company's values, select role models who exemplify the desired behaviors and deploy them in visible positions of authority. . . . Be generous and public with your recognition of their performance. . . . You will be making it clear that the path to success in your company is in emulating these behaviors.**

Reason 2

Some companies pursue a training solution instead. They seem to believe that if they communicate the desired behaviors in training sessions, employees will correspondingly adjust their daily behavior. As a stand-alone solution, training is foolishness. If high-profile managers and individual contributors do not engage in the desired behaviors, employees will accuse management of not "walking the talk." They will not be motivated to alter existing behaviors.

Reason 3

Other companies attempt to use behavioral coaching solutions or behavior-based performance appraisals to drive culture change. Again, it is difficult for employees to be receptive to culture change if the organization is dominated by role models who engage in behaviors that are inconsistent with its declared values. Unless high-profile managers consistently model the desired behaviors and actively recognize employees who engage in the behaviors, no real culture change is possible.

Reason 4

Many merged organizations select key managers based on a combination of qualifications, politics, and personality rather than qualifications and culturally desirable behaviors. This practice results in little or no consistency in the behavior of selected role models. Consequently, cultural integration is slow, if it takes place at all.

> It is difficult for emloyees to be receptive to culture change if the organization is dominated by role models who engage in behaviors that are inconsistent with its declared values.

Amid this emphasis on selection and deployment, it bears repeating that if the culturally desired behaviors are linked to defining events and value drivers, then they will produce economic results. Therefore, managers who exhibit the culturally desired behaviors are more than role models. They are people who produce results and drive shareholder value. Their effect on the performance of the organization is multiplied because others emulate their behavior.

From Rome to Rangoon

The CEO sounded desperate.

His multinational company had just absorbed a far-flung competitor, with outposts from Rome to Rangoon. Suddenly he had to assemble a whole new management team with a superb capacity to handle key operations that could make or break his career.

"I now have senior managers working for me in sixteen countries," *he wailed, "and I haven't a clue about which ones fit the operating style we need. I think I see the right style: the ability to respond quickly to market demands, a taste for innovation, a different way of thinking and communicating than we have now—but that's only half the battle. I have two hundred international managers out there—all strangers to me—and I can't trust my people to tell me who's right and who's wrong. If I pick the wrong people, or drive away the right people, I strengthen my competitors. I need outside perspective, honest information. I need help."*

The information this CEO urgently needed couldn't be found in a personnel file. He could scan stacks of résumés, review credentials, and weigh qualifications, but none of it would answer his paramount question about each candidate: "What is this person's operating style? How does he or she handle situations like the ones we're facing? Does he or she behave in ways I can predict and rely on?"

The usual criteria are perilous. Who's the right man to run Europe? Who knows? Presumably it's someone already there—the man running France, say, or Italy, Germany, Holland, or Switzerland. Maybe the one who speaks three languages and has an MIT degree? Maybe the one who has a great wife and looks presidential? On it goes, irrelevance after irrelevance.

And, of course, it turns out that the right "man" to run Europe isn't a man and isn't even in Europe. She's the brilliant chief financial officer of the Australian subsidiary, which seems to be buying everything in the Philippines. Her operating style is ideal for running European operations. Unfortunately, the CEO had never heard of her. Instead, he hired a German who looked like De Gaulle and drove the French clients crazy. Wunderbar.

And, of course, it turns out that the right "man" to run Europe isn't a man and isn't even in Europe. She's the brilliant chief financial officer of the Australian subsidiary, which seems to be buying everything in the Philippines. Her operating style is ideal for running European operations. Unfortunately, the CEO had never heard of her. Instead, he hired a German who looked like De Gaulle and drove the French clients crazy. Wunderbar.

Huge stakes ride on making the right deployment decisions, especially in the confusion of multinational mergers, acquisitions, and other large-scale changes. Nobody is in greater danger than the executive who's handing out billion-dollar responsibilities to managers he or she barely knows beyond names, titles, and useless personnel files. The wrong decision could easily destroy the decision-maker.

What this harried CEO experienced is all too common—and not just during times of transition. Making good selection and deployment decisions can turn a poor marketing plan into a successful advertising strategy or transform a hot new technology into a black hole of R&D funding. It can energize a workforce or destroy its enthusiasm. It can turn a foundering business into a rising star or a growing venture into an abject failure.

Few decisions have greater impact on culture and business success than the decisions on who will fill which roles. Mergers and acquisitions raise the stakes by challenging executives to make years of personnel choices in a few weeks. These choices not only set the tone for future staffing decisions but also have a profound impact on the operating style of the new organization. Despite the long-term consequences of these choices, the conditions under which they are made are far from ideal.

Misguided, guilt-induced attempts at democratic deployment end up resembling a quota system that violates every proclamation management ever made about the importance of merit.

Early in the process, managers begin jockeying for position. Executives either attempt to take care of their own people or bend over backwards to show impartiality by deploying as many of the acquired managers as possible. To make matters worse, their choices often are an attempt to balance the horse-trading and negotiating that began when the deal was struck.

Misguided, guilt-induced attempts at democratic deployment end up resembling a quota system that violates every proclamation management ever made about the importance of merit. Instead of a new organization populated with cultural exemplars, the result is an organization with too many people in jobs that can be neither defended nor comprehended.

There is an old Chinese proverb: "If you see a turtle on a fence post, you know someone put it there." In the context of mergers and acquisitions, it refers to people in senior positions who didn't get there on their own merit. These unfortunate and misplaced souls sit atop organizational fence posts, inviting uncharitable speculation about how they got there and whether they possess compromising photos of the CEO.

There's an old Chinese proverb: "If you see a turtle on a fence post, you know someone put it there." In the context of mergers and acquisitions, it refers to people in senior positions who didn't win these posts on their own merit. These unfortunate and misplaced souls sit atop organizational fence posts, inviting uncharitable speculation about how they got there and whether they possess compromising photos of the CEO.

Role Models: The Cultural DNA

It is always difficult to identify and select role models who will set the cultural standard for a company. It is even more difficult if this is attempted in the politically charged and emotionally laden atmosphere of a merger or acquisition. A major transition is not an environment conducive to thoughtful and even-handed decision making. Mistakes are made. And, the most common mistake is to treat selection decisions as simple choices about which of two people will fill one job. The second most common mistake is to rely on gut instincts—a good strategy for a food critic, perhaps, but a lethal one for a manager. Too often these instincts are influenced more by appearance, credentials, seniority, and

Shooters and Bashers

Many years ago an elementary school coach invented a game called boxing basketball. He put a pile of boxing gloves in the middle of the court. Each of his nine-year-old players was told to select one glove.

The rules were simple. Normal basketball with one exception. The kid who had the ball could get bashed as long as he held on to the ball. The coach was trying to teach teamwork and ball movement: the longer you held on to the ball, the more you got bashed.

A player could choose to put the glove on his strong hand or his weak hand. There were advantages and disadvantages. With the glove on his strong hand, he would be pretty good at bashing but have a harder time shooting. If he put the glove on his weak hand, he'd be good at dribbling, passing, and shooting but not very good at bashing.

At the beginning, most of the nine-year-olds put the glove on their good hand—bashing was the order of the day. The kids just didn't get it. After a while some players realized that winning the game was about making points, not bruises. So they switched hands.

The teams with more shooters regularly beat the teams with more bashers. They moved the ball around, avoided most of the bashing, and scored most of the points, while the bashers chased the ball around the court, trying to catch up with somebody to slam.

Eventually there were two kinds of teams: Shooters and Bashers. Shooters allied with shooters, and bashers allied with bashers. Shooters always won the games. But there were always teams of bashers.

It wasn't that the bashers couldn't become shooters. They just preferred bashing to winning.

In selecting people, the point is the same. It is not enough to know what they can do. You must also know what they will do—and, for that matter, prefer to do. Like kids playing boxing basketball, companies want people who will pass and shoot, not people who can shoot but prefer to bash.

political capital than by demonstrated ability to model behaviors consistent with the value drivers.

What matters most is what people *will* do, not what they *can* do. We all know people who can do something but don't. As China's late leader Deng Xiaoping observed more than three decades ago: "Yellow cat, black cat—as long as it catches mice, it is a good cat."

When it comes to filling the leadership ranks of a company, every CEO is looking for cats that catch mice.

It is not enough for a person to look the part, have impeccable credentials, and know all the right people. CEOs want people who produce results the way they want results produced. They want people who can be relied on to do the right things, the right way, at the right time. They want people who will think, act, manage, and communicate in ways that are aligned with company objectives and consistent with stated and unstated values.

These people carry the company's cultural DNA. They lead and teach by example. They are the role models. They are the cats that catch mice.

Finding Cats that Catch Mice

Following a merger or acquisition, the task of finding role models is all the more difficult because the role models don't congregate in one place. They inhabit both organizations. They can be found in every function and at every level. They may be long-service employees or relatively new hires. They come from diverse ethnic backgrounds and from all geographic regions.

Absent a comprehensive and efficient selection process, the search for role models will be short and shallow, or long and convoluted. Harried executives that are under intense pressure to make and announce key appointments, even prior to obtaining regulatory approval, do not spend time defining the desired culture before screening candidates for key positions. They look for candidates in obvious places, examine all the wrong information, and rely on their guts to make the final decisions. And consider for a moment the type of information they typically

> **The good people you don't pick leave with proprietary knowledge of your technology, products, and customers. They go to your competitors with revenge in their hearts. They leave behind stalled projects, demoralized colleagues, incomplete projects, and a learning curve for other employees.**

rely on to make these decisions— incomplete résumés, traditional interviews, outdated personnel files, and recommendations from politically minded managers. Even when the data are supplemented with additional interviews and updated profiles, the results reveal little about how well a person will perform and fit the desired culture.

By the way, the problem with résumés and traditional interviews—even competency-based interviews (a consulting fad)—is that they capture only what a person *can* do. They seldom reveal what a person *will* do or *prefers* to do. Given a choice between a person who can do the job and a person who also, will do the job, and prefers to do the job, the decision is simple. Select the latter.

The only reliable way to accurately identify cultural role models is to include behavioral interviewing in the candidate screening process. While there are many behavioral interviewing techniques, any systematic approach will suffice if it provides reliable information about the operating style and preferences of the individuals being considered for key positions. Absent these data, executives will be forced to bet their company's future on a leadership team selected largely on the basis of politics, personality, and social graces.

The Hidden Cost of Hiring Morons

Given the screening processes that are typically used, it is not surprising that the success rate for selecting the right people following a merger or acquisition isn't much better than the success rate for most mergers and acquisitions. What is surprising is that these perfunctory practices are allowed to continue. The impact of picking the wrong people and putting them in the wrong jobs often spells the difference between a transition that succeeds and one that fails. Mistakes at the top cascade down.

As one exasperated executive put it, "In all my years of hiring and firing, I've learned one important thing: first-rate people hire first-rate people, sec-ond-rate people hire third-rate people, and third-rate people hire morons."

> **As one exasperated executive said, "In all my years of hiring and firing, I've learned one important thing: first-rate people hire first-rate people, second-rate people hire third-rate people, and third-rate people hire morons."**

The good people you don't pick leave with proprietary knowledge of your technology, products, and customers. They go to your competitors with revenge in their hearts. They leave behind stalled projects, demoralized colleagues, incomplete projects, and a learning curve for other employees.

Deployment mistakes are always more expensive to fix than to avoid. They eliminate better candidates, drive off talented people, frustrate the achievers, undermine cultural integrity, and drive down performance. As the CEO of a software development company said: "We're trying to forge a new culture. The people we pick first are critical. Everyone will be watching what they do, what they say, how they manage. We get this part wrong, we get it all wrong."

Reinforce the New Culture

Once role models have been deployed in visible positions of authority, these exemplars of the new culture should be showered with recognition. This will position them as people whose behavior should be emulated. The message will be further reinforced if other employees who engage in the desired behaviors are quickly and visibly promoted, recognized, and rewarded.

> **Get everyone's attention early. The fastest way to alter a company's culture and raise the mean performance is by significantly rewarding the high performers.**

The speed of reward and recognition is critical. Get everyone's attention early. The fastest way to alter a company's culture and raise the mean performance is by significantly rewarding the high performers. Ignore the low performers.

By visibly providing substantial monetary rewards and nonmonetary recognition, the message of performance is loud and clear. Those who want the same recognition and reward will willingly alter their behavior and emulate high performers. Absent reward and recognition, those who are not willing to align their behavior will leave. Either alternative is desirable for the company.

However, rewards should not be limited to cash reinforcement. The reward for walking the talk should include influence and career opportunity, not just a few extra percentage points at pay review time or a larger bonus. If you fail to acknowledge the contributions of role models with the more valuable currency of influence and career opportunity, someone else will. Money whispers, influence speaks, and career opportunity shouts.

When a person walks away from a job, he or she walks away from a monthly salary. When that person walks away from a career, he or she forfeits organizational status, influence, and firm-specific knowledge, only to have to rebuild it in another organization. Short of abysmal compensation, few people really want to walk away from an organizational investment in their career.

The Final Factor: Muddled Messages Weaken Culture

Finally, the company's own policies and procedures can undermine culture change and integration. This occurs most often when there is a difference between a company's written policies and the behavior it rewards. For example, it is not unusual for a company to claim that product quality is its number-one objective and then reward employees only for quantity of product produced, regardless of quality.

Many companies make the mistake of preaching teamwork but rewarding only individual performance. Still others exhort their employees to be more innovative, but then criticize them for not following established procedure or, worse, punish trailblazers when they fail. This latter practice communicates that it's better not to try something new than to take a chance on trying and failing.

These deadly combinations of practices send muddled messages to the workforce:

"Be creative as long as you follow these detailed procedures."
"Produce quality product but get it out fast."
"Be a team player, but don't let your own productivity slip."
"Take chances, but don't make any mistakes."

Companies don't usually intend to send muddled messages, but misaligned policies create confusion nonetheless. The result is demoralized employees, increased turnover, reduced productivity, and delayed progress. Even if desired behaviors are identified, role models are deployed, and balanced incentives are provided, misaligned policies will undermine efforts to drive culture change.

> **We spend a lot of money hiring people who can think on their feet, and then we don't let them do it.**
>
> *Director of technology for a Silicon Valley microelectronics company, commenting on the inconsistency of hiring highly qualified, seasoned engineers and then requiring them to adhere religiously to design procedures that limit their freedom to think.*

■■■

Cultural incompatibility is neither the cancer of combinations nor the cause of failed mergers and acquisitions. Cultures can't be blended, changed slowly, or coaxed along with eloquent speeches. Culture change is rooted in behavior change, reinforced by role models, stimulated by incentives, and supported by sensibly aligned policies.

No tricks, no magic, and no rabbits pulled out of hats.

12

The Blind Man's Dog

Value Creation Incentives

Mergers and acquisitions are not just announced; they are trumpeted with great fanfare and enthusiasm. Competitive advantage and new business opportunity are confidently forecast, as if just saying it makes it so. Increased shareholder value is promised, and the entire venture is celebrated as a dream deal.

This hype generally includes the fantasy that the acquired management and technical team will cheerfully switch allegiance and enthusiastically align itself with the new strategies, structures, and processes. Everyone is expected to work together as a team. Generally within weeks of the announcement the dream deal morphs into the *Nightmare on Elm Street*.

Excitement evaporates early. As the hard work of execution gets under way, distraction and disruption supplant business focus. Commitment and enthusiasm wane. Recruiters court the company's most valuable employees, luring them to competing organizations.

The company is forced to offer sign-up bonuses, retention incentives, and other enticements to lock in key players. Promises

> **Golden parachutes and handcuffs become glittering anchors that induce inertia, obstruct progress, and destroy shareholder value.**

> **A fundamental challenge for executives, then, is the preservation of human capital, retaining and motivating people who will make a real difference.**

are made. Bidding wars ensue. Golden parachutes and handcuffs become glittering anchors that induce inertia, obstruct progress, and destroy shareholder value.

Assets—hard and soft—lose value quickly when the managers who know how to leverage them depart—either in body or in spirit. Key people often leave with core technology, crucial customer relationships, proprietary knowledge, vendor and industry relationships, and the loyalty of other employees who eventually follow them. These departures disrupt business, distract the organization, induce uncertainty, and lower productivity.

A fundamental challenge for managers, then, is the preservation of human capital, retaining and motivating people who will make a real difference. Savvy dealmakers know that after an acquisition it's wise to settle executive and key contributor compensation quickly. In a sea of distractions, matters of compensation can quickly become tidal waves.

How to Reward Diminished Value: A Morality Tale

This is a story about an acquisition that began with a commitment to hot technology and bright hopes. It ended with a hollow shell, lagging behind competitors.

A Fortune 100 company, with mature products, stiff competition, and aging technology, acquires a small company with patents on an exciting technology but still undeveloped products. Successful introduction of the new products will transform the industry and catapult the combined company to market leadership. An infusion of investment capital is necessary. A significant acquisition premium is necessary to do the deal.

To make the deal economics work, the acquired company must maintain its present customer base, meet ambitious cash-flow goals, and deliver the new product in fewer than three years. The technical and operational challenges are significant. The acquiring CEO knows that the new company cannot risk any turnover among the key players.

In a bid to hold on to key people while the deal is being negotiated, representatives of the acquirer make casual references to sign-up bonuses and special incentives. A few loose tongues wag about million-dollar awards. The COO attempts to ingratiate himself by agreeing that the acquired team is entitled to rewards proportionate to those of Silicon Valley's most notable entrepreneurs. The deal is primed for catastrophe.

Amid handshakes, dinners, and promises to iron out the details after the deal is closed, the top managers of the small company start fantasizing about how they will spend their soon-to-be-received, and obviously well-deserved, fortunes. Discussion rapidly turns to new homes, Ferraris, and tropical vacations as casual daydreams grow ever more opulent.

After the deal, however, the perceived offers seem to lose their urgency, and questions about promised incentives get only vague responses from the acquiring company's management. The acquired management team becomes obsessed with whether the promises will be kept, how much they will get, and when. Talk of intellectual property ownership, venture capitalists, and career alternatives pushes aside concerns about customers, technology, and operational priorities.

Months later the acquiring company launches a compensation study, but by then resentment is rampant. The acquired company's performance is declining. Complaints about unreasonable cash-flow goals are frequent. New-product development is falling behind schedule. A key technical manager leaves to join a smaller competitor offering a lower salary but significant equity. Worry over who might leave next fuels rumor, speculation, and a betting pool.

The acquirer finally completes the compensation study and submits it for board review. The incentive package is generous to a fault, with attractive sign-up bonuses and an impressive five-year retention incentive. The impending disaster could be averted at this point, but the board balks. They ignore the CEO's pressure to approve the plan. They are afraid that shareholders will view the plan as a giveaway.

Enter the legal teams. The acquired company's managers argue that the parent company has reneged on a commitment. Lawsuits are filed— but not before several more key players pack their bags. Customers, too, begin to leave, migrating to more stable competitors. Adding fuel to the growing conflagration, progress on the new product is negligible.

The attorneys agree that litigation can be avoided. After heated ne-
gotiations and several marathon meetings, the lawyers agree on a new
incentive plan. Payouts anticipated under the plan are well in excess of
those originally denied by the board. Performance requirements under
the plan are much lower and tied only to cash flow—completely disre-
garding the fact that the company's future and its only hope of recover-
ing value resides in launching the new product.

Legal fees are mounting. Cash flow is falling disastrously short of
projections. Institutional investors are raising questions. Management

---

Sooner Is Better

The PricewaterhouseCoopers mergers and acquisitions survey found
that 77 percent of participants who implemented effective long-term executive incentive plans within the first three months of their transitions
also reported more energetic and enthusiastic management and greater
clarity and confidence among employees about the company's direction.

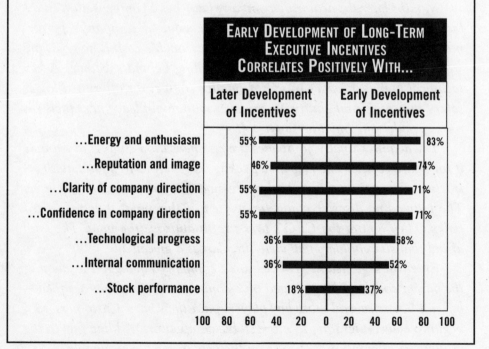

EARLY DEVELOPMENT OF LONG-TERM EXECUTIVE INCENTIVES CORRELATES POSITIVELY WITH...

	Later Development of Incentives	Early Development of Incentives
...Energy and enthusiasm	55%	83%
...Reputation and image	46%	74%
...Clarity of company direction	55%	71%
...Confidence in company direction	55%	71%
...Technological progress	36%	58%
...Internal communication	36%	52%
...Stock performance	18%	37%

100 80 60 40 20 0 20 40 60 80 100

pressure is increasing. The board feels trapped. A phenomenally costly incentive plan is approved.

The rest of the story reads like a dime novel. The company couldn't overcome the inertia that had set in during the legal battle. Performance and market share continued to deteriorate. An alternative technology was introduced by a competitor. Shortly thereafter, the parent company negotiated a deeply discounted leveraged buyout with the management team.

Dear Mr. Herzberg . . . Get a Life

The relationship between incentive compensation and company performance sounds intuitive. However, in 1959 a researcher named Frederick Herzberg published a now-famous study of motivation in the workplace. He concluded that money isn't a motivator. For many years thereafter academics solemnly repeated that refrain. Then, over the past decade, a small army of fringe academics and consultants began to argue that rewards and incentive plans reduce enthusiasm, creativity, and quality of work.

This is like being told not to use a knife because it might cut your finger. Good advice for five-year-olds, clumsy people, and incompetent jugglers. Bad advice for butchers, cooks, and anybody who has to whittle a company into shape for a living.

There is no intent here to diminish the considerable investment these righteous folk have in their hypotheses. But stop and think for a moment.

Look at the rate at which CEOs jump ship for better deals in other companies. Consider the annual struggle over employee pay increases in most companies. Consider the power of stock op-

Picture a casino in Las Vegas. Hundreds of gamblers stand at hundreds of slot machines, but the average person is interested in only the numbers and pictures that come up on the machine he or she is playing. Why? Because he or she has a stake in that machine.

tions to drive intense commitment in venture capital start-ups. Consider the ease with which technologists of all kinds leave secure positions for the options offered in a risky start-up. Witness the growth and spread of premature IPOs.

Picture a casino in Las Vegas. Hundreds of gamblers stand at hundreds of slot machines, but the average person is interested in only the numbers and pictures that come up on the machine he or she is playing. Why? Because he or she has a stake in that machine. Managers are no different. The bigger their stake, the more intense their interest, and the more they will stretch to capture the rewards.

Does anybody out there really believe that money doesn't motivate? If money doesn't motivate, maybe at least we can agree it has a miraculous ability to get people's attention. And after all, in most businesses this is exactly the purpose of incentives: to energize effort and focus behavior on achieving end results.

The Blind Man's Dog

While standing on a street corner one day, waiting for a traffic light to change, a psychology professor noticed a blind man with a guide dog trying to cross the street.

The dog began to lead its master into the intersection before the light turned green. Tires screeched, horns honked, and bystanders gasped. Flustered, the blind man backed up onto the curb. The dog started off again—screech, honk, gasps. Finally, on the third try, the dog successfully led its master across the street.

As soon as the man stepped onto the opposite curb, he reached into his pocket, retrieved a treat, and gave it to the dog. Puzzled by the man's action, the professor walked over and said, "Excuse me, but I'm a professor of psychology, and I just saw what happened. If you reward the dog for what it just did, it will never learn the correct behavior."

The blind man thanked the professor for his concern, but explained, "I'm not rewarding the dog. I'm just trying to find out where his head is so I can beat the hell out of the other end!"

Unfortunately, the architects of most corporate incentive plans make

Are You Squandering $432,000 Every Day?

One of the biggest barriers to higher productivity is lack of direction and enthusiasm. Focused, energized employees are not only more pleasant to have around; they're more productive—25 percent more productive by some research estimates. If a company has one thousand employees and pays each of them an average of $45,000 per year in salary and benefits, the cost of wasted labor alone could run as high as $43,269.23 per working day. In terms of revenue, the number could be three or four times higher.

Incentive plans designed to energize and focus behavior on actions that drive economic value are a proven antidote for the lethargy and distraction that so often poisons a company following the announcement of an acquisition, merger, or significant change. If a company has ten thousand employees, taking this medication might be worth $432,692.30 per day!

the same mistake the professor did, they take an academic approach rather than a practical one. They are often preoccupied with funding formulas, eligibility criteria, delivery mechanisms, tax treatments, and administrative requirements. The plans become Rube Goldberg–like contraptions that defy logic, frustrate managers, and confuse participants. They lose sight of the real objective: to energize and focus behavior.

There is an old business saying: "What gets measured gets managed. And what gets managed gets done." A more appropriate motto might be: "What gets rewarded gets done." To get people to behave in ways that support the value drivers—that is, to focus on the 20 percent of actions that are going to drive 80 percent of the value of the transition—rewards need to be aligned with what needs to be accomplished. The

> **Unfortunately . . . most corporate incentive plans . . . become Rube Goldberg–like contraptions that defy logic, frustrate managers, and confuse participants. They lose sight of the real objective: to energize and focus behavior.**

sooner the appropriate reward plan is put in place, the smoother the transition.

Value creation incentive plans (VCIPs), which are contingent on incremental shareholder value creation, offer a potentially elegant solution to the problem. Often referred to as "equity simulators," these customized plans are self-funding, high-stakes, simple-to-communicate, attention-grabbing incentives.

"We need hard-charging, fire-breathing designers and engineers who are willing to put in long hours to get winning products on the market quickly," said the CEO of one of the world's largest electronics manufacturers.

Discussing the company's incentive plan for its development team, he added: "If these guys can meet deadlines and produce a winner, they'll get a piece of the pie. The more successful the product, the bigger the pie."

The small development team was located in the heart of the Silicon Valley. Its charter was simple: develop a new video chip to strengthen the parent company's position in a very competitive segment of the consumer electronics market. Because the team's leaders were being wooed by competitors and venture capitalists, the parent company's most pressing issue was to keep the team intact and focused on a very tight design schedule.

The team was already distracted by organizational uncertainty, and competitors were rapidly developing their own video chips.

To keep the team from breaking apart, the company needed an incentive plan that would both retain and motivate its key members. The plan would have to provide significant opportunity with less risk than would be demanded by venture capitalists.

The value creation incentive plan designed by the company called for an unlimited pool of cash funded by operating income. Team members were granted shares of the pool according to their roles in the company and their success in meeting developmental milestones. They also had the option of buying additional shares.

A minimum value would be assigned to the shares when the new *video chip was released into production. Participants could then sell the shares back to the company or hold on to them. Retained shares would increase in value and earn annual dividends. Top team members could earn up to $1.5 million in less than five years if the rosiest projections were met, and a senior designer could expect to collect up to $600,000.*

Simply handing out shares reinforced the design team's efforts, but the monetary reward was contingent on producing a successful video chip.

These types of plans are called *equity simulators* because they mimic some of the risks of ownership and the rewards of equity without actual shares or options. This helps to align employee interests with shareholders' interests while not diluting equity. Moreover, unlike stock options or phantom stock, VCIPs are not subject to the vagaries of the stock market. An option may be underwater, but a value creation incentive opportunity can still pay out if measurable value has been created.

VCIPs allow management to give participants an opportunity to earn significant sums at little or no risk to the company. They pay out a small portion of the incremental value created—usually defined as cumulative cash flow from operations—over an extended period of time, typically three to seven years.

Developed for high-growth, high-technology companies in the early 1980s, VCIPs can help large companies keep key contributors from fleeing to small start-ups, while motivating strategic project teams to accelerate the development of critical new products.

The concept is a simple one: produce an incentive pie out of the incremental shareholder value that will be created under the accelerated transition sce-

VCIPs offer a reward for meeting specific objectives proportional to the value created for the company.

nario. Give managers and key individual contributors slices of the pie based on their contributions to incremental value. That may involve meeting strategic development milestones, achieving market penetration objectives, reengineering operations or processes, meeting revenue growth and profit objectives, and so on.

A distinctive feature of VCIPs is their ability to link payout to value creation and encourage achievement of specific goals. The plans reinforce effort, then pay out for results. Unlike traditional goal-oriented plans, they offer a reward for meeting specific objectives proportional to the value created for the company. This overcomes a common incentive dilemma: how to attach incentive value to interim accomplishments that don't, in and of themselves, have any measurable economic value.

The trickiest part of designing a value creation incentive plan is the funding formula. The actual contribution rate must balance the risk and return to shareholders with the opportunity cost and compensation level for the participants. It's usually done by modeling various performance scenarios and then establishing a contribution rate that has a reasonable chance of funding the incentive pool if value creation objectives are met.

One Company's Approach

After development team members at a large electronics company received shares in the incentive pool, they could invest their own money in additional shares. Funding of the pool came from a percentage of income from operations. There was no cap on the size of the pool.

When new products were released, shares achieved a minimum value, and members could sell their shares back to the company. Shares that were held, however, continued to grow in value and earn annual dividends based on the commercial success of the project. A key executive's shares could be worth more than $3 million in fewer than five years. A designer could accumulate more than $500,000.

The plan neither ensured business success nor guaranteed retention of key people. It was an incentive vehicle that offered significant value without fixed compensation cost. The message was simple: "Meet deadlines, get a winning product released, and you get a stake in the jackpot. If the product succeeds, the pot will get really big."

During the plan's first few years, shares in the incentive pool are distributed to key managers and individual contributors based on how well they achieve major objectives. Until the cumulative cash flow from operations—or some other measure of shareholder value creation—exceeds a minimal return level, the shares have no value. Participants who want to cash out vested shares can sell them back to the company, thereby forfeiting future appreciation. Incidentally, the early cashing out of shares by participants alerts management to potential leadership problems in much the same way that liquidation of stock by officers raises similar concerns.

The success of VCIPs depends on how effectively the incentive architects address certain challenges.

Rewarding Economic Value Creation: Six Challenges

1. Keeping the Objective in Focus

Although retaining and motivating valuable employees is a critical issue, the primary objective is to focus behavior on value creation. It's not enough just to hold on to good people. You want to keep good people performing in ways that enhance the company's value proposition.

The cornerstone of these plans is the list of value-driving initiatives generated by the leadership team (see chapter 5). Since the purpose is to reward behaviors that drive value, these value drivers become the specific objectives and milestones that determine incentive opportunity and trigger payout.

2. Linking Incentive Payout Directly to the Creation of Economic Value

The most effective retention incentives are those that are linked directly to shareholder value. This can be accomplished by creating a self-funding pool that represents a modest percentage of the value that will be created for shareholders over a three- to five-year period.

Usually participants earn shares in this value creation pool for timely achievement of strategic objectives. The earn-in feature reinforces early action by providing an attractive noncash reward—that is, shares in the incentive pool. The number of shares that can be earned varies with each participant's ability to influence results.

At the end of the performance period, payout is based on the actual value created; plan participants are entitled to cash out the value of the shares they've earned. Ultimately there must be parity between the value and liquidity of the benefits that accrue to the corporation and the value and liquidity of the rewards.

3. Avoiding the Setting of Maximum and Minimum Opportunity Levels

The fear of a windfall payout to participants often provokes management to cap what someone can earn from a plan. While this tactic may ensure that unearned rewards are limited, it also communicates a negative message. Capping extraordinary payouts is demotivating to participants and discourages extraordinary effort.

Another common mistake is to guarantee a minimum payout. Sometimes, when business conditions are difficult, a company attempts to "protect" participants by establishing very low performance thresholds or adjusting targets after the fact. This guarantees some level of payout. Though well-intentioned and fair-minded, such a tactic can backfire. First, it shields executives from the sharp edge of failure. Second, it lets them off the accountability hook for the goals set for the company.

4. Requiring Participants to Make an Investment

When participants are forced to make investments that carry a risk of forfeiture, retention is strengthened. Having a stake to protect makes them more willing to persist in the face of setbacks and obstacles. And since long-term success often requires overcoming many setbacks, knowing that key players have an added reason to persevere is reassuring to shareholders.

A high-stakes incentive plan is more palatable to investors if the participants have made a tangible commitment. Participants can be asked to accept reduced salaries, to forfeit other incentives, or to make personal cash investments. This also is a useful way of testing commitment.

5. Keeping the Plan Simple and Straightforward

Creating an incentive plan that is easy to understand does not mean that it must be simplistic or inflexible. Simplicity does not ensure elegance. When "keep it simple" becomes the overriding design rule, the result is often an overly streamlined plan that fails to meet any other objective. On the other hand, the temptation to create a monument to incentive design is often overwhelming. In an earnest effort to come up with the best plan possible, it's easy to forget that brilliant design isn't the objective.

> When "keep it simple" becomes the overriding design rule, the result is often an overly streamlined plan that fails to meet any other objective. On the other hand, . . . in an earnest effort to come up with the best plan possible, it's easy to forget that brilliant design isn't the objective.

A sophisticated plan must meet multiple objectives, reinforce a variety of behaviors, and address numerous constraints; thus it cannot, by definition, be simple. It will be complex. The communication challenge is to keep it from becoming confusing. Focusing the communication message on what participants want to know rather than on what management thinks they ought to know helps achieve this goal.

6. Sponsoring the Plan

The speed of the design process and the ultimate quality of the plan are directly related to the level of sponsorship. Doors open, data flow, schedules are freed up for meetings, and attention is captured if sponsorship comes from the board. Likewise, early involvement from the board speeds the final approval process.

Incentive Plan Communications
(Challenge 5)

Most participants have only a few key concerns:
  How much can I get?
  When can I get it?
  What do I need to do to get it?
  What is the likelihood that I will get it if I work hard on
  the right things?
If the answers to these questions are lost in a lengthy communication document, no matter how well crafted, motivational value will be the victim.

In the End, It's Not Just Money

Too often retention of key managers and individual contributors is seen exclusively as a reward issue. Yet, when the reasons for turnover are examined, the primary cause is often found to be a perceived reduction in the ability to influence decisions. For example, executives in an acquired company are generally disheartened by the loss of autonomy. Whether the source is anxious bankers or expectant investors, executives are likely to feel overmanaged. Even those who report a hands-off attitude by the new ownership frequently groan over new reporting requirements and constraints imposed on decision making.

Although a VCIP may help retain and focus key employees, it will not offset the perceived loss of freedom to act. It also is important to provide influence and career opportunities. In offering a complete package of income, influence, *and* career opportunity, the company can increase the level of enthusiasm and improve the odds of retention and motivation.

Implementing VCIPs alone won't guarantee that the company will succeed or that key employees ultimately will not leave. However, a properly designed and implemented plan can provide a powerful inducement that will energize and focus behavior on value driving actions. It will help retain talent and will speed the capture of incremental shareholder value.

13

The North Bank

5:00 A.M. *The alarm rings. Startled, John Woodstock, CEO of Global Computer, begins flailing about in an attempt to locate the snooze button on his clock radio. Glasses, papers, and a watch scatter across the bedroom floor as his arm connects with the top of his nightstand. He scrambles out of bed, the clock beeping even louder. Finally, he grabs the little beast and pushes the button with both thumbs. Out of breath, heart racing, and head pounding, he looks around the room. Rome? Seattle? Malaysia? Home? The painting on the wall resets his bearings. Home.*

He staggers into the bathroom, swallows three aspirin and drinks directly from the faucet. That was the most exhausting night of sleep he can ever remember. John mumbles to himself "Global-Nexus may be a great deal, but I may not live to see it work."

He wonders if Johnny Wu lost any sleep last night. Or his investors. Or his customers. Or his employees. Or that pain-in-the-ass reporter from the Mercury. *Bet not.*

John pulls on his robe, fumbles with his watch, and heads for his den by way of the kitchen. Just enough time to make coffee before the 5:30 A.M. conference call with London and New York.

He sits down at his desk, leans back in his chair, and sips the black coffee. He looks at his watch: 5:22.

*He looks down at the top of his desk. Squarely in the middle of his blotter sits a neatly clipped document resting on top of the opened Federal Express envelope. Attached to the first page is a sticky note from his assistant that reads, "For the conference call tomorrow A.M." In bold letters the cover announces, "**Preliminary Draft, Letter of Intent, Nexus Acquisition.**"*

John leans forward. Letter of intent? What's going on here? He sets down his coffee cup and thumbs through the document. Then he looks at the date. June 5. But it's late September! He starts to panic. He looks at his desk calendar. June 5. He looks at his watch. June 5.

I've completely lost it, he thinks to himself. This is it, I'm suffering from global transient amnesia! It's next June, and I've lost track of nearly nine months! He looks back at the document. No, the year is the same.

I've visited the future? Not possible. What's going on? His mind starts racing. It's June 5, not September? We haven't signed the letter of intent? How could this be possible?

John sits back and tries to sort out the thoughts colliding in his head. The mental fog begins to clear. He must have had a dream—correction—nightmare. The Global-Nexus merger disaster has not happened.

No calls have come in from impatient customers demanding to know when the new products will be released. No mass exodus of software developers. No acerbic analysts forecasting doom. Even the gnawing in his belly has disappeared.

John's confusion gives way to relief. He hasn't lost control. The game hasn't even begun. There's still time to maneuver.

The phone rings.

> **Most acquirers are repeat offenders, not because they enjoy pain, but because they are under tremendous pressure to grow. Done right, growth by acquisition beats the pants off of growth by other means.**

John Woodstock, CEO of Global Computer and future "dealmaker of the quarter," didn't journey through time, isn't suffering from global transient amnesia, and hasn't experienced a psychotic episode. He's under too much stress and hasn't been getting enough sleep. And last night he challenged his stomach to a duel over jumbo shrimp, a thick steak, and baked Alaska. His stomach won and his subconscious lost. The punishment was a nocturnal visit from the Ghost of Deals Lost.

Like many CEOs about to make the deal of their career, John suffered from a full-scale anxiety attack. Though relieved to discover that it had all been only a nightmare, he still had a tough decision to make. Should he go through with the Nexus deal or not? And if he did, how would he avoid the disaster he dreamed about all night?

The odds are that executives like John Woodstock will go through with their deal. Most acquirers are repeat offenders, not because they enjoy pain, but because they are under tremendous pressure to grow. Done right, growth by acquisition beats the pants off growth by other means.

Deals are high-risk propositions with potentially huge payoffs. Even though most are done at a conceptual level, they are not done without forethought or trepidation. Most executives are sensible people. They usually don't put their company, career, fortune, and family in harm's way on a whim. The consequences of failure are long-lasting and frequently fatal.

No company has ever downsized itself to greatness or backed its way into market leadership. Luck has never proved to be a sustainable strategy.

Gaining a competitive advantage and leading the market offer many rewards to those with the courage to try and the skills to succeed. No company has ever downsized itself to greatness or backed its way into market leadership. Luck has never proved to be a sustainable strategy.

The principles of an accelerated transition presented in this book represent not a growth strategy but rather a means of implementing a growth strategy. The Accelerated Transition® is an integrated proposition for getting a company from point A to point B with as little disruption and destruction as possible. It is a buyer's protection plan.

As discussed in previous chapters, the basic principles are simple:

1. Base the transition strategy on the economic value drivers.
2. Aggressively manage communications in order to secure stakeholder support and acceptance.
3. Launch small, fast-paced, short-term transition teams that will accelerate implementation of the value drivers.
4. Align organizational roles and responsibilities to ensure clarity of direction.
5. Build a behavior-based culture around defining events dictated by the value drivers.
6. Select and deploy role models who support the desired culture.
7. Link incentives directly to the creation of shareholder value.

The specific techniques for implementing these principles are less important than adherence to the complete proposition. The full, positive effect can be achieved only when all the elements are addressed in a cohesive manner.

Growth is a continuing process of building up and tearing down, of combining businesses and breaking them apart, of changing direction and staying the course. The trick is to create an organizational capability for rapidly adapting to the ever-changing competitive landscape. Those who learn faster, act quicker, and adapt sooner reap the rewards first. Those governed by fear and gripped with caution must share whatever is left over.

The Accelerated Transition® is not a formula, prescription, or cure-all. It isn't an insurance policy against failure or a guarantee of success. It's an integrated set of concrete actions with as much failure filtered out as experience will permit. This approach enables senior managers to gain the competence, confidence, and courage they require to navigate any transition with speed and focus.

So, put your foot on the gas and follow that big value-driving bus across the raging waters, and don't forget to wink at Carlos and his buddy as you pass.

Welcome to the North Bank, amigos!

Index